ONE WEEK LOAN

JAMES PENROD is Professor of Dance at the University of California, Irvine. He has choreographed and performed nationally and internationally in concerts, musicals, operas and on television. He is a specialist in movement analysis and currently is a movement consultant and choreographs for California Dance Visions.

JANICE GUDDE PLASTINO heads the Performing Arts Medicine Program at the University of California, Irvine. In addition to serving on the faculties of several universities and the American Dance Festival, she has directed opera at Lincoln Center, and has performed at the Edinburgh Festival and on national television.

Both Penrod and Plastino toured and danced as partners nationally and internationally with the dance company they formed in 1971, the Penrod Plastino Movement Theatre.

The Dancer Prepares

MODERN DANCE FOR BEGINNERS

Fourth Edition

James Penrod
Janice Gudde Plastino
University of California, Irvine

Mc Graw Hill

Boston   Burr Ridge, IL   Dubuque, IA   Madison, WI   New York
San Francisco   St. Louis   Bangkok   Bogotá   Caracas   Kuala Lumpur
Lisbon   London   Madrid   Mexico City   Milan   Montreal   New Delhi
Santiago   Seoul   Singapore   Sydney   Taipei   Toronto

McGraw-Hill Higher Education

*A Division of The **McGraw-Hill** Companies*

THE DANCER PREPARES, FOURTH EDITION

Published by McGraw-Hill, a business unit of The McGraw-Hill Companies, Inc., 1221 Avenue of the Americas, New York, NY, 10020. Copyright © 1998 by The McGraw-Hill Companies, Inc. All rights reserved. No part of this publication may be reproduced or distributed in any form or by any means, or stored in a database or retrieval system, without the prior written consent of The McGraw-Hill Companies, Inc., including, but not limited to, in any network or other electronic storage or transmission, or broadcast for distance learning.

Some ancillaries, including electronic and print components, may not be available to customers outside the United States.

This book is printed on acid-free paper.

6 7 8 9 0 DOC/DOC 0 9 8 7 6 5 4 3 2

ISBN 1-55934-675-2

www.mhhe.com

Library of Congress Cataloging-in-Publication Data
Penrod, James.
    The dancer prepares : modern dance for beginners / James Penrod. Janice Gudde Plastino. — 4th ed.
      p. cm.
    Includes bibliographical references. (p.) and index.
    1. Modern dance. I. Plastino, Janice Gudde. II. Title.
GV1783.P44 1997
    792.8—dc21
                                          97-18848
                                              CIP

    Sponsoring editor, Serina Beauparlant; production editor, Melissa Kreischer; manuscript editor, Mary Roybal; text and cover designer, Jean Mailander; illustrators, Kristin Mount and Robin Mouat; manufacturing manager, Randy Hurst. The text was set in 10/13 Minion and printed on acid-free 50# Finch Opaque by R. R. Donnelley & Sons Company.

    Cover Photo © Lois Greenfield, 1990. Pilobulus Dance Theatre, Dancers: Adam Battelstein, Vernon Scott, John Mario Sevilla, Kent Lindemer.

    Illustrations based on drawings by Robert Carr.

    Additional photo credits appear at the back of the book on page 98, which constitutes an extension of the copyright page.

Contents

Preface

Movement never lies. Everything that a dancer does
on the stage tells the audience what he is.
—MARTHA GRAHAM

This book is written for you who are taking your first course in modern dance to introduce you to the content of the course and to explain to you your role as a student. The authors assume you have little or no background in the art or technique of the dance.

No one can be taught how to be an artist, but you can be taught the craft of an art form. We hope to help you discover a new appreciation of the arts in general and to inspire in you a desire for self-discovery, self-discipline, and eventually self-expression in the art form of dance. This book introduces you to rudiments of the dancer's craft such as basic techniques, dance clothes, and the care of your body. It also discusses choreographic fundamentals and evaluation procedures. We hope these objective principles will help you form a subjective ideal that will inspire you to commit yourself more fully to the dance world.

Why you have decided to study modern dance is of little consequence. The important thing is that you have enrolled in a course to learn the most exciting of the movement forms. You have chosen a course that is physically rigorous and exhausting, mentally stimulating and exasperating, and creatively exciting and frustrating. It is probably one of the most self-satisfying courses that you will take. We do not assume that you will become a professional dancer, although we have directed the ideas in this book toward that goal. We do, however, hope you will experience the joy of movement well-executed, the exhilaration of creative endeavor, and the appreciation of dance—the most fleeting of the art forms.

This book is concerned primarily with the analysis of modern dance techniques, combinations, and vocabulary. Although it is written for the beginning student, the book contains information that will be of value to the intermediate student as well.

This edition has been updated and expanded with practical, theoretical, and historical information that will increase the usefulness of the book. Chapter 2, Preparation, includes updated information on preparation. Chapter 4, Anatomy, Injuries, and Diet, includes updated information and the current scientific opinion on the warm-up and the cool-down. Chapter 5, History, has been expanded to include contemporary choreographers and trends of the 1990s. Chapter 6, Improvisation, provides additional information about the improvisational experience and process and self-awareness. Chapter 7, Choreographic Approaches, has been expanded and includes more information on music and internal-external focus, and Chapter 8, Evaluation and Criticism, has been expanded. The Selected References section has been updated. New photographs have been added as examples of historical and contemporary work of choreographers and companies.

We do not intend to preach a philosophy or theory of some ephemeral art form that can be mastered by reading statements about how to dance. We do intend to deal with concrete, specific, practical matters relating to the mastery of the creative and technical aspects of dance.

We would like to acknowledge the following individuals for their assistance: Kirsten K. Barron, Mary Corey, Rita Marks, Michael Munoz, and Lorelei Tanji. We would also like to thank the reviewers: D. Barber, Pasadena City College; Jo Dierdorff, Riverside Community College; Paula Frasz, Northern Illinois University; Patricia Ann McClanahan, Sinclair Community College; David Ollington, aha! dance theatre, Kansas City, Missouri; and Candace Winters-March, Western Illinois University, as well as the many other teachers who have suggested ideas for the book; and the University of California, Irvine, Department of Dance for its support.

Chapter 1
Introduction

Love the art in yourself, rather than yourself in art.

STANISLAVSKY

Bebe Miller Company, "The Hendrix Project." Photo © 1995 Lois Greenfield.

DEFINING MODERN DANCE

Now that you have enrolled in your first modern dance class, which might be called something like Modern, Contemporary, Creative, Freestyle, Dance 40A, or PE 5B, you may be wondering just what modern dance is. Modern dance is comprised of highly individualized movements based upon personalized, ever-changing artistic standards. The innate nature of modern dance provides for constant redefinition of the field by practicing artists/dancers. In America two different concepts of modern dance were identified by two early pioneers, Doris Humphrey and Martha Graham. Humphrey identified fall-recovery as the falling away from and the returning to equilibrium. Graham identified contraction-release as exhalation and inhalation, respectively, as the basis for all movement (in Germany Mary Wigman used the term *die and arise*). These concepts formed the basis of many of the movement concepts used in modern dance.

A Blend of Techniques   In the past, "modern dance" represented the viewpoints and movement concepts of each of several dancers or choreographers. For example, there was the particular modern dance technique of Graham, of Humphrey, or of Wigman. As the horizons of the dance artists have widened, the various movement forms have become more alike. In the past, it was easy to recognize ballet by its codified positions and movements. This is no longer true. Today many "ballet" choreographers utilize the movement concepts of the modern dancer, and many of the body placements and exercises of the ballet dancer are now used in the "modern" techniques. Many choreographers now include in their work not only the elusive modern dance techniques but also the principles of jazz and ballet, and adapted styles from dances of world cultures.

If the term *modern dance* is to be defined for today, it should be broad enough to include all of the diverse approaches existing now and likely to exist in the future.

What Dance Can Do for You   Perhaps more important to you than a concise definition of what constitutes modern dance is what it can contribute to the enrichment of your life. Modern dance can help give a grace and poise to all your movements and contribute to your general sense of well-being through the pleasure of a well-toned body. It can introduce you to a new form in which you experience the joy of movement and compete solely with yourself. It can heighten your appreciation of music, the plastic arts, and all movement forms. It can increase your respect for and understanding of the dancer's profession. And, finally, a modern dance course will expand your awareness and appreciation of the way you and others move.

DANCE AS A CAREER

Hopefully, some of you will be inspired by your modern dance experience to choose dance as a career. Dedication to the art of the dance *might* require you to forsake money, fame, and even family in order to reach the pinnacle of artistic success in the dance world. Many sacrifices are involved in such an aspiration, often without the longed-for rewards. After five to ten years of dedicated work, you may not yet be accepted into a dance company. Even if you are accepted, the company may be unable to pay you a living wage. You often must be prepared to support yourself by means other than dancing. Because the financial rewards are so low, living conditions may be barely adequate and certainly will not be luxurious. The hardships involved in giving concerts or arranging performances of your own works can be heartbreaking as well as rewarding.

Yet under such trying circumstances the art of dance flourishes. Dedicated, disciplined people continue to expand the vocabulary of movement. New forms are continually created in the artist's push forward. The hope of making a contribution to the understanding of life keeps the search for success alive.

Perhaps dance does not appeal to you on that level. Perhaps you have seen the beautiful women and handsome men, dressed in the latest fashions, who dance across television or movie screens. Such "Hollywood dreams" are within the realm of possibility. But you must decide whether you are willing to make the commitment necessary to attain them.

There have been and will continue to be those few dancers who have extraordinary luck and who obtain a good job without too much hard work. This happens rarely and in the long run usually leads to undesirable results. Almost always, these dancers fail because an inadequate background and bad training have failed to prepare them for the next job. It is risky to let yourself be talked into accepting a job before you are ready. If your training is to be interrupted or stopped by a job, then think twice before you take that job. Performing experience should be a part of your dance education, but it should supplement training, not take the place of it.

Anyone who is dedicated to a dance career must be prepared to work hard. You probably will perform before you have had five years of training, but you should continue to return to the classroom to keep your body in top condition. If you become a dancer, your body will be your working instrument, just as a violin is a violinist's instrument. Unlike the violinist, however, the dancer must build the instrument while learning technique and the skills needed to perform.

Like an Olympic athlete, the dancer should be dedicated to acquiring the greatest skill possible—not for financial gain or simply to win, but for the satisfaction of giving his or her best. No less than a devoted athlete, the dancer must be disciplined and dedicated to this high purpose.

Although women choreographers and dancers still comprise the majority in the field, men choreographers and dancers have and do make significant contributions. Almost equal numbers of women and men choreographers continue to produce works, but more women are available to perform. As is the case with most forms of dance in the United States, men performers are in the minority. Thus, the field of modern dance is full of professional opportunities for men dancers.

In addition to careers in performance and choreography are many related careers: teaching at all levels and for all ages, dance notator, reconstructor of dances, dance therapist, historian, critic, journalist, accompanist, stage technician, stage manager, video artist, dance computer specialist, multi-media performance expert, arts administrator, company manager, fund-raiser, dance publicist, dance agent, dance producer, public relations specialist, movement analysis specialist, dance medicine/science specialist, dance trainer, expert in one of the allied movement therapies such as Pilates-based technique, Alexander, Feldenkrais, or Bartenieff technique, dance orthopedist, performance-stress expert, and costume, set, and/or lighting designer. This short list gives you ideas to pursue in your love for the art, as all of these specialties are necessary for modern dance to exist as a performing and developing art.

Modern dance can offer a diversion or a way of life—either a brief introduction to one of the most exciting of the art forms or total dedication to a life's work. The choice is yours.

DANCE FOR VIEWING

As a dance student, you should attend dance concerts to see the finished product that was started in the studio. It is often difficult to see a live professional performance unless you live in a large city or near a university that sponsors touring companies. The alternative is to see professional performances on film and television. Many excellent films and videotapes of dance exist and can be ordered for a small fee. Commercial television seldom offers first-rate concert dance, but it does offer entertaining dance by exciting, competent performers and choreographers. Educational and public television often show new works as well as older works of leading choreographers. Many universities have fine companies or performance dance groups who offer exciting, creative productions. It is to your advantage as a student to see dance, whether good or bad. You can always learn something at a dance concert, even if it is only what not to do.

Dance Audiences   While interest in all forms of dance is rapidly growing in the United States, the audience for modern dance has traditionally been smaller than audiences for other art forms. There are several reasons for this. One is that modern dance is a relatively new art. In contrast to opera and ballet, which are often supported financially by established society, modern dance is thought by many people to exist only for the benefit of other artists and dancers. This is unfortunate. Modern dance reflects the time in which it is danced. It is usually contemporary, because it is created by and for those who are interested in the reflection of life today.

Another reason modern dance has not enjoyed a wide following is that using the human body as a medium for art formerly carried a stigma. The Puritan influence fostered the belief that the sinful body should be hidden from view; only the mind and soul were worthy of serious study. More recently, the human body has become more acceptable as an appropriate medium for artistic expression. The belief that dancing bodies are sinful now exists only in certain sections of our society, and even there this view is changing.

Audiences and Finances   Many modern dance artists and their companies are beginning to enjoy limited financial support as they become acceptable to the general public. One artist who did a great deal to promote the acceptance of modern dance was Martha Graham. Her success came slowly and only after many years of work and dedication. She achieved her greatest success as a performer and choreographer in the late 1960s, in her seventh decade. Graham retired as a dancer in 1969 and died in 1991.

But even famous artists such as Martha Graham cannot maintain their companies on audience support alone. Most of the established professional companies are forced to rely on private foundation money or government grants. Stipulations are sometimes imposed on the person who accepts these funds. These demands may hinder or help the artist. It would be to everybody's advantage if the companies could be supported by the audiences who attend the performances.

Certainly the size of an audience is not always the best measure of the quality of a work of art. Artists are often ahead of their times. One criterion of the caliber of the artist is the ability to see new trends and to synthesize these insights in a new way. Therefore, works of art may not evoke a response from people who have not been introduced to the situation as the artist has interpreted it.

Filming and Preserving the Dance   The development of the video camera has had a profound impact upon modern dance. It has made all kinds of dance easily accessible for the first time to the viewing public. Public television stations now broadcast performances of modern dance companies almost weekly to all areas of the United States. High-speed, low-light video cameras have made it easy to record all levels and forms of dance. Original works can now be preserved for viewing by later generations. Before the advent of the video camera, dance works were often performed only for a season or two and then forgotten except for still photographs and the memories of the performers and the fortunate audiences who had seen the live performances.

In addition to the video camera and playback equipment, comprehensive dance notation systems such as Labanotation and Choreology-Benesh have been developed in this century. These systems provide a written dance symbol language that is now being used to preserve great dance works in a manner similar to that for musical scores. The video camera records an individual performance on videotape just as music is recorded on a record, cassette, or compact disc. The dance notation score preserves the dance work as near as possible to the original intent of the choreographer. Those trained in one of these notation systems can learn dances and analyze choreographic structure and style from the scores.

Chapter 2
Preparation

The human body is an instrument for the production
of art in the life of the human soul.

ALFRED NORTH WHITEHEAD

Momix Baseball. Photo by Moses Pendleton.

Like the centuries of dancers who have gone before, you are embarking on one of the most exciting experiences of a lifetime. Even if your dance training consists of only one course, you will be awakened to an unlimited range of body movements. You will dance about those things that concern all people everywhere—the search for an awareness of what it means to be alive, to create, and to begin to understand humankind and our place in the universe.

Having enrolled in a modern dance class, you might be asking—as many students do—a series of questions: What should I wear? How should I wear it? What happens in a dance class? How much do I need to know about music? All these are good questions, and the answers will help you get the most out of your classroom experience.

This chapter provides general answers. To learn the special requirements of your course, check with your teacher or a representative of the class. Some teachers like to use the first class meeting as a discussion period, so you should find out in advance whether ordinary clothes or dance clothes should be worn to the first session. If you have any unanswered questions, ask them! Most teachers are used to answering questions and are happy to help. Teachers of modern dance are dedicated, knowledgeable, and creative and want you to have an inspiring experience. Questions and answers can enhance your learning.

CLOTHING

Special Requirements   Often the beginning dance student wonders why in most dance studios students are asked to wear special formfitting clothes for dance classes—clothing that could be thought of as an outer skin. There are several reasons.

Dance is a visual art that uses the dancer's body to create architectural designs in space. Any clothing that does not conform to the outline of the body will alter the designs created in that space. Some students might ask whether this isn't desirable in some cases. The answer would be an emphatic yes. Clothing can evoke an era, enhance some movements, and give a new look to the movement and the spatial design that a silhouetted body alone could never achieve. Students in a basic technique class, however, are not usually concerned with these issues, unless they are experimenting to find new movements inherent in the restrictions imposed by the costume.

The second reason for special clothing is that the main concern of classroom technique is to align your body in a series of exercises that will strengthen and stretch it in order to make it responsive to the physical demands that will be made upon it. The teacher must be able to see the placement of your body in order to give an intelligent criticism of your work. Guessing as to what you might be doing under piles of clothing is dangerous! Faulty placement of your body in exercises will weaken and even injure you if you repeat it often enough. You could compare an overdressed dancer to a building that is covered with unnecessary exterior frills that hide its basic structure.

Dance clothing also puts you in the proper frame of mind to work in the dance class. A person usually associates certain activities with a certain kind of clothing. For example, when you swim, you wear a bathing suit. Clothing that restricts movement prevents proper exercising in the same way that ordinary clothing restricts the movement of a swimmer in the water. When you are dressed in clothes worn only while dancing, you soon associate the clothing with dancing, which, in turn, helps put you in the mood of the experience to come.

Today's simple dance costume has evolved over many centuries. The first dance costumes were styled after the clothing worn every day by the dancers in the courts of the sixteenth century. The women wore long, full dresses that hid their bodies and prevented freedom of movement. As time passed and more technical demands were made on women dancers, their dresses were shortened to permit freer movement. Men's costumes also were simplified until finally a simple leotard was introduced in the mid-nineteenth century by Jules Léotard, a famous French acrobat. At last dancers could appear without voluminous piles of cloth that restricted and hid movement.

In the ballet, women eventually wore the long "romantic" skirts or the short "classical" skirts that we associate with the "white" ballet today. They also wore toe shoes that allowed them to rise onto the tips of their toes to evoke an ethereal, romantic quality in their movements. Modern dancers broke with this tradition to use simple tights and leotards or free-flowing gowns and bare feet, which allow more freedom of movement.

Sometimes students or their parents think the wearing of dancers' tights is immoral. Consider the clothing worn on the street today! Tights are modest by comparison. Tights, leotards, or the one-piece unitard could be compared to contemporary bicycle shorts, running tights, or ski racing pants—all appropriate to their activity.

Most dance schools require special clothing. This clothing can be purchased in dance boutiques or department stores. Check with your teacher before purchasing shoes, tights, or leotards. If the teacher requests shoes, they can be ballet slippers or a modern slipper that leaves the toes and heels exposed. Most modern dancers do not wear shoes while dancing. For various reasons, aerobic clothing is not usually worn in modern dance. Check with your teacher.

Women's Clothing   Women usually wear tights that cover the legs and hips and a leotard worn under or over the tights that covers the hips and trunk. If tights are seamed, the seam is worn in the back. Panties or a girdle may be worn under the tights, but under no circumstances should these garments be allowed to show. The showing of the outline of the panty beneath the leotard destroys the long look of the leg. If you feel uncomfortable without panties, perhaps a brief bikini panty will suffice. A well-fitting bra should be worn by anyone with a breast size above 32A. Breast tissue can be torn away from the underlying musculature if the breasts are not properly supported.

Stirrup tights are preferred, although some dancers still choose tights with feet cut off at the ankle or opened along the sole. The latter can also be worn for other types of dance classes that require shoes.

With the popularization and purchase of dancewear by the general public, many styles of leotards in many new materials have become available. Likewise, clothing worn for aerobic and fitness workouts sometimes influences new dancewear. Dancers seem to delight in finding different ways to wear dance garments. The only rule to remember is that your body must be visually free and clean. Within this rule, almost anything goes.

Menstruation is a natural body process that a woman experiences approximately 350 times in her life. If the dancer regards it as a natural phenomenon, it should cause no problems. She should participate in dance class with no hesitation during the menstrual period. If she feels sluggish or slightly uncomfortable, she will probably feel much better after the class. Often, stretching can relieve cramps. Even if she has pain associated with the onset of menstruation, she should not miss more than one class a month. It is too difficult to catch up in the class. It must be stressed that, if a woman is contemplating dance as a career, missing class is not acceptable. There will be many times when she must audition or perform with cramps or other unpleasant sensations associated with the menstrual period. It is to her advantage to learn to work at such times.

Sometimes a student is embarrassed at having to wear a pad under a tight-fitting leotard. A tampon might relieve her distress. The tampon is undetectable when in place and does not interfere with movement. The use of a tampon is a matter of personal preference, of course. The main consideration is to be comfortable and at ease during the menstrual period. Whatever helps a student enjoy the dance class is acceptable.

Men's Clothing   Men's clothing consists of tights pulled up firmly in the crotch to avoid a baggy, droopy-drawers look. The tights are usually of a heavier, less sheer material than women's tights. The seams are worn in the back. A dance belt is worn under the tights to hold the genitals firmly in place and to help prevent ruptures. The one-piece dance belt, about the same size as jockey shorts, gives more support than the athletic supporter ordinarily worn under gym clothes. Of the two belt styles available, one is similar to a formfitting swimsuit, and the other, an elastic-cloth thong style, is designed to be worn with the wide cloth (spandex) part in the front. Belts are available in white, black, and suntan. The line of the belt should not show through the tights, and the belt should be the same color as the tights for the same reason.

Tights should never hang down in the crotch and distort the body line, a fault that is a clear indication of a beginning student. Male dancers frequently hold up the tights with an ordinary belt around the waist, then roll the tights down over the belt. Others hold up the tights with clip-on suspenders or with elastic bands sewn onto the tights and carried over the shoulders as regular suspenders. The suspenders give a better line in that they eliminate the bulky belt line. A tight-fitting, waist-length T-shirt is worn over the torso. This can be tucked into the tights or can hang out if it doesn't cover the pelvic area. For both men and women, the tights and accessories should be worn so that the line of the body can be seen clearly.

Some dance schools allow dancers to wear biker shorts or leggings rather than having to invest in special clothing. The main drawback to shorts is that they do not protect your legs while you are doing floor work and do not keep the body heat concentrated in the legs, which helps keep the muscles warm. Also, they are not as aesthetically pleasing to the body line as tights are.

Clothing Variations   Tights and leotards are produced in many colors. Some schools insist on uniformity in the colors worn by students. Check with your teacher before buying colors other than black (worn by both men and women) or pink (customarily reserved for use by women). If you are allowed to choose your own colors, consider what colors do to the look of your body. If you want to make your body as attractive and slim-appearing as possible, black is for you. Darker colors will make you look slimmer. Lighter colors are better on a slim body. If you wear colored tights, it is preferable to wear subdued tones. Remember that bright, garish colors tend to make you look larger. The top and the bottom of the outfit should blend harmoniously. A severe contrast in colors tends to chop the body visually into two sections, which is generally not flattering. Some dancers prefer to wear warm-up garments over their leotards and tights. Some teachers object to these layers of clothing because they distort the line of the body. Check with your teacher about the recommended or required clothing for your class before purchasing and wearing warm-up garments.

Care of Clothing   Dance clothing can be expensive, but it will last for years if properly cared for. Dance clothes should be laundered *after each wearing,* either in warm water alone or with soap and water, in order to prevent fading, rotting, and odor. Hanging tights to dry, rather than using a dryer, will help maintain their condition and original size. They should not be stored in a locker when wet with perspiration. When tights develop runs, they should be sewn as soon as practicable in order to ensure a longer life for them. In addition, good hygiene and common courtesy dictate a shower after each class.

PERSONAL APPEARANCE

Hairstyles   If your hair is long, it should be secured in such a way that it does not fall over your face or into your eyes. It is extremely distracting to the dancer to have hair that insists on its own creative endeavors, and it is distracting to the audience too. You should find a hairstyle that is attractive and yet practical for dance.

Accessories   Before entering the classroom, check to see if you have with you all the accessories that might be needed: extra bobby pins, elastic bands for the hair (never for the shoes, as the bands break and present a hazard to everyone working), shoes if required, notebook and pencil if requested. If you perspire heavily, a towel is a good classroom accessory. Those who wear glasses can purchase at a sporting goods store a strap to hold them securely in place. Since glasses are not worn in performance, some dancers purchase contact lenses. Some teachers allow you to use knee pads. If they are allowed, it may be easier to work with a thin padding than with a thick one.

You should be prepared for any clothing emergency that might come up once the class work has begun. It is disturbing to the classroom continuity and to your concentration to be forced to leave the room or stop to adjust clothing. Preparation for such contingencies is the beginning of self-discipline.

Fully prepared, you put on the dance clothes and then walk into the studio to follow in the footsteps of a tradition that spans the centuries. This tradition relates to the basic needs of the primitive tribesman, the courtier of the royal courts, and even the sophisticated club dancer ecstatically moving to the pounding rhythm of the latest club music.

CLASS PROCEDURES

The Dance Studio   As you walk into the studio, you are quite likely to see a fairly large room with cylindrical wooden railings (called barres) attached to the walls. The dancer uses these to maintain balance while doing exercises. Some studios use a portable barre, while others do not use barres at all. In the front of the room you might see a large mirror or series of mirrors covering one wall.

Some teachers have you face the mirror so that you can visually see what you are doing. Others have you face away from the mirror so that you can begin to sense what your body is doing without reliance on the mirror. Both approaches have value in your training. The first allows you to get visual feedback about your own body lines and postures. The second prepares you to become kinesthetically aware of where your body is in space.

The floor is usually of hardwood that gives slightly under the weight of the dancer's body, thereby preventing injuries and lessening fatigue. Many professional dancers refuse to dance on concrete. The floor should never be waxed or finished with a lacquer, as most gym floors are. The floor should be washed with water only—never with a cleaning agent. Soaps leave a film that makes the floor slippery. The floor should be free of splinters, nails, and small holes. Some floors are covered with marley, a covering designed for dance.

Warm-up and Cool-down   As you look around, you probably see people dressed in tights, some holding onto the barre, others seated on the floor, all warming up their bodies with simple movements before they begin more strenuous physical activity. Warm-up is probably the most important technique for a dancer to learn. It not only helps protect the body from injury but also prepares the body and the mind for the actual dance class. Although many teachers include a specific warm-up in their classes, it is your responsibility to prepare your own body for the class. All bodies are different; some take longer than others to respond to exercise and to be ready to dance. The method of warm-up should include easy stretches (never bounce in a stretch of any kind), a full range of movement in all of the joints, and easy large-muscle movements so that the core temperature of the body rises. The body temperature may be raised by easy jogging around the studio, by floor work that uses the entire body in a progressive manner, or by gradually increasing the intensity of reaching and bending. When you have produced a light sweat over your body, you have evidence that you have prepared the body to begin to move as your teacher asks.

The cool-down is as important at the end of a vigorous class as the warm-up is at the beginning of the class. This is the perfect time to do easy stretches in a static position, engage in slow walking around the studio, or perform movement for the entire body that is slow and sustained. You should wait until you have stopped sweating before showering and/or leaving the warm studio without several layers of clothing.

General Procedures   When the teacher walks into the room, he or she may be joined by a pianist who will provide the music for the class. Other teachers use a hand drum to set the rhythm that you will dance to. Or perhaps recorded music of some kind will provide the accompaniment. The accompaniment will vary according to the individual preference of the teacher and, more often, the financial backing of the department or school.

The teacher calls the class members from their separate areas of the room, and thus begins your participation in the dance, which the philosopher Havelock Ellis, in *The Dance of Life,* calls "the source of all the arts that express themselves in the human person." In your new adventure, you will explore the natural rhythms and physical movement possibilities of your body.

Every class has a basic rhythm or form to it. Often the class starts with the warm-up, then moves into the controlled exercises that strengthen your body and develop technique. Usually these exercises are preparing you to do some specific movements for the class on that day. Once you start the class, don't sit down, as your muscles will get "cold" and you could injure yourself. Usually the exercises become more vigorous as the class progresses. Some teachers prefer to end the class with jumps or big movements; others prefer to work the class "down" with tranquil movements so that when you leave you are not as emotionally "high."

Some teachers use the barre in their exercises; others do not. Some teachers do exercises only on the floor or standing; others rarely use the floor. All methods and approaches are valid. All teachers are working toward the same goal, which can be attained in many ways—the goal of helping you develop a beautiful and artistically expressive body.

Demonstrations   The teacher will begin the class by demonstrating movement patterns for you to follow. Some teachers may not demonstrate but rather will "talk" you through the movement. Unless the teacher specifies that you are to do the movement in your own way, try to copy the teacher's way. An important part of dance training is developing your "artistic eye" to see all the nuances of movement and then reproducing them as demonstrated. There are several reasons: Correct execution of an exercise is imperative if injuries are to be avoided and physical control is to be established; mastery of the body is part of the satisfaction that comes from dancing; and those who want to be professional dancers must be able to learn movement patterns quickly and correctly. The dance world is highly competitive and without large financial resources. The choreographer who must produce a work in a limited amount of time, sometimes as little as one week, is forced to hire well-qualified, well-trained dancers who learn quickly and correctly. Dancers who can do any movement required of them by the choreographer are usually hired first. You cannot learn to dance on the job.

Improvisations   Sometimes the teacher, rather than demonstrating a movement pattern, will ask you to improvise movement. If asked to improvise, listen carefully to the movement image given by the teacher. Don't try to intellectualize, plan the movement, or reproduce a movement that you have learned in the classroom. The chief values of improvisation are to free your body with movements that are natural to yourself, to encourage you to be spontaneous, and to stimulate your kinesthetic memory and imagination. Sometimes, to stimulate the senses or the imagination, the teacher will ask you to recall a mood, a physical or emotional state of being, or movement patterns in space and time or to imagine how it would feel to be someone or something.

If you can allow yourself to enter into the spirit of the improvisational experience, you will find it very rewarding. It may be the area of movement where you discover whether or not you want to be a dancer, teacher, or choreographer.

Decorum   A few commonsense acts of classroom courtesy will make the class function better for all participants. Do not talk in the classroom except to ask or answer questions. In order to avoid accidents, be aware that you are sharing the dance studio with others. When the teacher organizes the places where you stand in the room into lines or some other arrangement, listen to the instructions. When you are asked to move across the floor, line up and wait your turn as instructed. A lot of time is wasted if the teacher has to keep answering the same questions because someone did not listen to instructions or to an answer. Be alert and attentive—you will gain more from your dance experience.

Attendance   Students usually know how to study in a regular academic class, but many are at a loss over how to get the most out of a dance class. One of the most important things you can do is to attend every class.

Reading a book, this one included, will not teach you how to dance or how to be an artist. You need the daily movement experience in order to make progress. A crash program in last-minute physical exercises before the final examination will reward you only with fatigue. If your school does not give a final movement examination, then you will probably be graded on your progress in your daily classroom work. If you are given a final movement examination, it will usually deal with the areas of movement that you have learned in class and will be evaluated according to how well you understand and execute the movements. Whether you are given an exam or graded in the class, you can take out of the class only what you have gained as a person and as an artist. The pleasure of the experience and self-development should take precedence over grades, even if you are going on to graduate school.

Observing Movement   When the teacher demonstrates an exercise, watch carefully the flow of the movement and the exact positions the whole body and individual parts of the body take in space. Next, try to move through the exercise by physical suggestion of the positions rather than an all-out physical effort. This will develop your kinesthetic sense or motor memory—fancy terms meaning simply the physical sensation you experience when you watch someone move, for example, in skating, dancing, falling, or jumping. Then try to do the movement as completely as possible. Watch the other dancers do the movement when you are not working and see if they are doing the same thing the teacher did. Watch the students who move well; ask yourself why they move well and apply their approach to your own movement. Watch the students who do not move as well, and ask yourself why they are not as successful in the exercise. Observing the teacher, other students, and yourself trains your artistic eye to see the design of line, shapes, forms, and movement patterns—all elements of dance. Listen to and apply immediately the criticisms your teacher gives you, as well as those given to the class in general. The criticism is offered to help you. It is not an attack on you personally but rather a criticism to help you master technique. Your teacher is another pair of eyes working for you.

Developing a critical artistic eye is important to the dancer, but a word of caution is in order. Asserting that you know more than the teacher or other students is counterproductive in the classroom. Offer your opinions only when they are asked for.

Having an open mind to any and all movement is extremely important to the dancer. This presupposes a cooperative spirit with the teacher and with others in the classroom. A negative, noncooperative attitude will destroy the efforts of any teacher or fellow artist. A wise teacher—one who knows when to be firm and when to be light in approach—will encourage cooperation and a healthy climate of rapport. Good teachers recognize that intractable discipline and prodding are valid only when they benefit a potential talent. Your teacher will welcome intelligent questions and comments. You will gain the most from your classroom experience if you contribute to a spirit of cooperation and helpfulness.

MUSIC

In demonstrating an exercise, some teachers count out 1 2 3, 1 2 3 4, 1 2, or some other combination of numbers. Each number corresponds to a certain position that the body or its parts assume in space or move through in space. When you are asked to repeat the movement, you should attempt to arrive at these positions on the counts the teacher has indicated. The counts are then repeated in the music that accompanies the dance sequence you are doing. Some teachers "sing out" the musical pulse with sounds, words, images, or dynamic instructions to reinforce and stretch your commitment to perform and express the creative potential of the movement, not just to do a set exercise routine.

Other teachers will give you a phrase of movement that is to correspond to a like musical phrase. A phrase is a certain number of counts or positions that usually make a simple statement. The movement phrase can be likened to a sentence or fragment of a sentence within the spoken language.

A few teachers prefer not to use music, phrases, or counts. They attempt to get you to move so that you sense your own movements in a prescribed or nonprescribed time. Whatever method or methods they use, you should know that dance is done in time as well as in space, and you should understand what happens when the same movements are done slowly and fast. It is important to develop your own musical sense and a feel for movement rhythm, spatial rhythm, and dynamic rhythm.

In general, rhythm has to do with the recurrence of certain elements that establish the character of the movement and movement flow. Movement rhythm is your own phrasing of the movements, which may or may not be performed in time to the musical structure when you are dancing to music. Spatial rhythm refers to the spatial patterns or pathways you establish as you move through the dance. Dynamic rhythm is the quality of the movement established as you use greater or lesser energy to perform a movement. Your innate or conscious choices are what make your movement unique to you and establish the style and character of your movement.

In most cases, dance is performed to music or another rhythmical accompaniment, so a basic understanding of common musical forms can be helpful. You will be expected to "keep time" with the music. Studying a musical instrument or taking a beginning course in musical theory will help your dancing by developing your musical appreciation and knowledge. You can develop your rhythmical sense, which will help you move in time to the beats, by listening to all kinds of music and tapping or clapping out the rhythmical pulse (beat) you feel. As an added exercise, try to analyze the structure of the musical piece. You might ask yourself such questions as how the composer has divided up the musical beats you feel, what kind of musical phrases he has used, what moods he has suggested, or what kind of transitions he has used to move from one mood to another mood. Later you might want to study specific musical forms such as the waltz, polka, or mazurka and try to identify the characteristics of these musical forms. If you like the modern sounds of the club dances, you might enjoy trying to analyze the structure of these pieces. Try to decide why this music has such a universal appeal. Is it the insistent repetition of a basic beat or the subtle, shifting rhythms? Or is it the words?

Beat   There are some basic musical structures with which all dancers work, so you should have some understanding of them. When you watch someone unconsciously tapping his foot in time with a piece of music, he usually is tapping the floor in unison with the heavy accents in the music. These are the strong beats that keep the dancers or musicians moving or playing in unison. There are also light beats (subbeats) that precede the repetitious heavy pulses in the music. A light beat occurs when the person you are watching lifts his toes from the floor. A heavy beat occurs when his toes strike the floor. (See Chapter 7 for more information regarding standard accent patterns in different meters.)

Preparation Count   Part of the pleasure of your classroom experience will be the thrill of exploring with your teacher the various rhythmical possibilities and also the qualities and forms of movement. When the teacher has demonstrated and led you through a movement combination, he or she might say something like "ready and one." "Ready" is your warning to ready yourself to move. "And" tells you to set your body in motion to move into your first position on the count of "one."

All class exercises begin with a preparation count by the teacher. This preparation count tells the accompanist and the class in what tempo the exercise will be danced. This tempo might be different from the one in which the exercise was demonstrated or marked. In most modern dance exercises, the count corresponds to the last few numbers of the dance phrase. If the phrase, for example, is eight counts long, the preparation will typically be "seven and eight and." If the tempo is fast, four counts might be used: "five six seven eight." If the tempo is slow, one count may suffice: "eight and a." In all cases, the class usually remains motionless, prepared, and in the starting position of the exercise until the first beat of the initial phrase (the first "one").

Translating the rhythms and moods of the music into movements in space and time leads you toward the discipline that you must acquire if you are eventually to express to an audience your pleasure in moving. The same discipline will permit you to express your thoughts and feelings in dance. If you choose dance as a career, the discipline will help you contribute to your art as a dancer, choreographer, or teacher.

Breath Rhythm   When you are learning dance for the first time, many elements demand your attention. At times the demands can seem overwhelming, physically binding your movements so that you stop breathing and moving with natural ease. One basic element in dance that will enhance your movement and aid your freedom of movement from the beginning is learning about your own rhythm of breath inhalation and exhalation and how it supports you and the movement you are doing. As you are learning and doing new movement sequences, be aware of where your inhalation and exhalation give you a chance to exert yourself and then to recuperate from the exertion. What breath rhythm works for you? There are many elements—including breath rhythm—in the beginning classes to be mastered, but eventually your efforts will reward you with a sense of exhilaration in the sheer joy of movement and expression.

Self-observation   Your teacher is essential to your dance education, but ultimately you are going to get out of your dance experience what you are willing to invest in it. It is very useful to keep a journal recording your own observations of yourself. There are many self-reflective questions you can ask and answer in your journal:

1. Why are you taking this class?
2. What are your expectations?
3. What are your goals?
4. What do you want to accomplish and learn?
5. What are you accomplishing?
6. What do you need to work on for improvement?
7. Are you looking at yourself objectively both for the positive things you are doing and for the areas in which you know you can do

better?

8. Are you observing other students, as well as doing your best work so they can learn from you?

9. Are you being genuinely receptive to new movement ideas and concepts being presented in the classroom, ideas that might lead you to new perspectives and visions?

Your best preparation for dance is your spirit, enthusiasm, and commitment.

Chapter 3
Technique Analysis

What we do not understand, we do not possess.

GOETHE

Lar Lubovitch Dance Company, "So In Love." Photo © 1994 Lois Greenfield.

DEVELOPMENT IN TECHNIQUE

The development of modern dance as an art form came about by the breaking of the "rules" of what dance was "supposed" to be. The traditions and techniques of modern dance continue to evolve as new gifted artists change the rules. Such change is a healthy thing. An art form can grow only when new ideas and new modes of expression come into it.

One exciting element of modern dance is the distorted use of lines, shapes, and forms to achieve a new aesthetic of beauty. Any line, any shape, any form that the human body can assume in space is valid to the modern dancer if it expresses what the dancer wants to communicate. Some beginning dancers may think the movements they are asked to do are "ugly." If you should feel that way, think of the movements as a challenge to see if you can find any similar shapes and forms in the world around you, and then try to understand their validity in an art form.

Basic Alignment   You should be aware of a few basic points about natural body alignment in order to understand the deviations from it. Think of your natural alignment as "good posture." Think of your body as being lengthened upward from your foot support through the top of your head. The alignment is as if you were holding onto a bar over your head and hanging down from it. Think of a straight line running down from the top of your head through your neck, torso, pelvis, and legs. This line is the central axis of your body. When you are standing, jumping, kneeling, or sitting in a good posture, be aware that your head, chest, and pelvic area stay in a straight vertical line. Your shoulders should be comfortably directed sideward and downward.

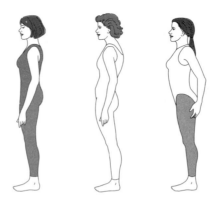

People with bad posture may slump forward so that their shoulders are rounded or may release their pelvis backward, causing a swayback. Avoid both distortions of line.

The following illustrations provide a few ideas for you to consider in your basic alignment.

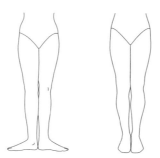

You should hold good alignment through various degrees of *leg rotation*. The legs can be either turned out from the hip socket or held so that the feet are pointed forward in a parallel position.

You should have *weight placement on the feet* evenly divided in a tripod between the big toe, the little toe, and the heel. When you rise to the ball of the foot (to half-toe), your weight should be between the big toe and the second toe, never toward the little toe.

Good alignment of the leg is essential to support in a *knee bend*. You should keep the center of the knee in line with the middle toe. In the small knee bend (demi-plié), the heels usually remain on the floor. In the deep knee bend (grand plié), the heels usually leave the floor naturally, in order to prevent a pushing backward in the pelvis with a subsequent lean forward in the torso. In the turned-out side position (second position) the heels usually remain on the floor.

To *balance on one leg*, lengthen upward on the vertical line through the body. Don't "sit" into the supporting leg. Shift the hip toward the supporting leg and on a slight diagonal upward. In the basic balance on one leg, keep the two front pelvic bones straight across on a horizontal line.

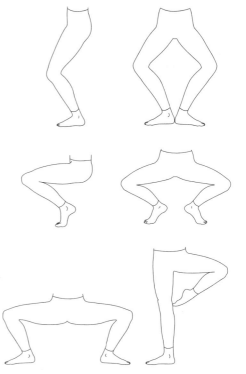

Terminology In general, modern dancers have not codified the terms for positions and movements. A number of modern dancers feel that codification of terms would inhibit free expression and prevent new forms of technique from developing. Another argument against codification is the infinite variety of positions the body can assume in space. Any code of modern dance movement would have to be limited and arbitrary. We have attempted to give names to body positions *only as a guide* to analyzing the infinite movement possibilities of the body. The names should be thought of as a springboard to further exploration and body analysis, not as an attempt at definitive codification.

Use of terms varies from one teacher to another. Learn the terms your own teacher uses so that upon hearing instructions you will be able to respond with the desired movement. For the purposes of analysis, definitions of basic positions are desirable. Then you as a student can both identify each basic position and understand the further development of that position. This helps you learn faster and helps train the "artistic eye" to see the subtleties of movement.

FIRST ANALYSIS

Movements in a Stationary Position While in a stationary position, you have only a few basic possibilities of movement: You can bend (tilt), rotate, shift, or support yourself in various ways. Despite the limited number of basic movements, however, many variations are possible, and a stationary position presents opportunities as well as restrictions. The drawings on this page and the next page show a few of the variations.

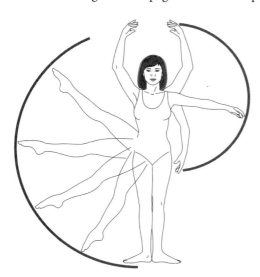

The *whole leg* can bend from the hip socket and move in any direction, to a certain level, with or without rotation in the hip socket and with or without a bend in the lower leg. The first illustration indicates various levels of the arm and leg in the side direction. The leg is limited in the degree of level it can achieve, but flexibility in the shoulder socket allows the arm to make a full circle (360 degrees), passing through the various levels in the side direction, as well as forward or back.

The *foot* can stretch forward to a "pointed" foot position or bend back to a "flexed" foot position, with or without rotation. The *arm* and *hand* have more freedom of movement but are similar to the leg and foot in bending with or without rotation. The *torso* can bend in any direction with a rounded back or straight back, to a specific level, with or without body rotation.

Bend (tilt)

The bend, or tilt, can be in the chest or pelvic area (more limited bending) or from the hip joints (greater bending). The *head-neck* can bend in some direction that is independent of the position of the torso.

The *torso* and its individual parts can all rotate around their own axes separately or together. The individual parts of the torso—*head, rib cage,* and *pelvis*—can do a kind of rotary action forward, backward, and sideward. The motion is more of a rocking action as opposed to the bend or tilt of those parts. The whole body can revolve completely on its own axis (turn).

Rotate

The *head, shoulders, rib cage,* and *pelvis* can shift as a unit from their central axis in some direction.

Shift

The *body* can be supported on the floor by sitting, kneeling, lying, or standing. It can leave the support by jumping or by being lifted and held.

Support

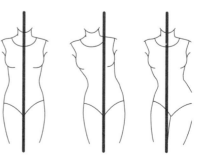

As a means of movement and position analysis, you could ask your-self various questions. Concerning *bending,* you could inquire: What part of the body is bending and to what level? Is the bend curved or sharply angled?

About *rotation* you could ask: What part or parts are rotated and in what direction? If the whole body is turning, is it a complete turn or only a fraction of a turn? Is the turn on one foot or both feet? What is the position of the body in the turn?

As for *shifting,* you could raise two questions: What part of the body is being displaced and in what direction? Is the shift only a basic impulse to move into another position?

And about *support* (or nonsupport) of the body you could ask: Is a new body support achieved by jumping or rising upward to the balls of the feet? Or is it arrived at by sinking downward to small or large knee bends or positions of kneeling, sitting, or lying? What positions are moved through to arrive at the new support?

Dance is, of course, more than just stationary positions. Dance involves moving the whole body through space from one position to another. The motivation behind the movement will change the look and feel of the movement.

SECOND ANALYSIS

Body Lines   Three basic lines can be achieved in dance. These lines may be formed by parts of the body or by the dancer's entire body, as shown in the illustrations opposite.

Vertical or horizontal lines are formed when the dancer stands upright, bends at a right angle, or lies on the floor. Such lines also may be achieved in many other ways.

Oblique (slanted) lines are formed when the dancer bends at an obtuse or an acute angle in relation to either a horizontal or a vertical. Oblique lines may be formed in many ways.

Curved lines are formed in various positions. These lines may be combined with the others, just as oblique lines may be combined with horizontals or verticals or both.

Because line is so important in the dance, you should visually trace the line of movement your teacher demonstrates and try to approximate it. Sometimes you may think another line looks better or feels better for you, but remember that part of the self-discipline of learning the dance craft is to make your body do anything that choreography requires.

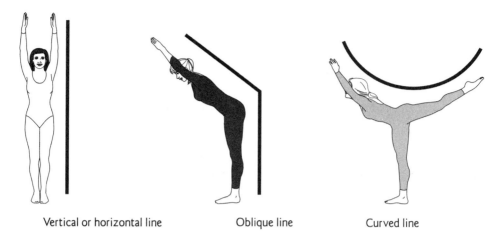

Vertical or horizontal line   Oblique line   Curved line

THIRD ANALYSIS

Feet Positions   Many modern dancers use some version of the following feet positions, with the legs either parallel or turned outward or inward from the hip sockets. These illustrations indicate the usual degree of turnout for the beginning level:

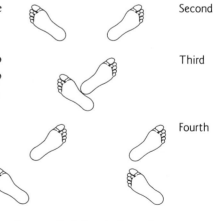

In the *first* position, the heels are together (closed).

First

In the *second* position, the heels are about twelve inches apart (open side).

Second

In the *third* position (closed heel to instep), the front heel is next to the instep of the back foot, and the feet are touching.

Third

In the *fourth* position, one foot is about twelve inches in front of the other. The heels may be in line (not crossed over), or the heel of the front foot may be in line with the toes of the back foot (crossed over—open forward-backward).

Fourth

This closed position is sometimes called the sixth position. Also, the open fourth can be opened to a diagonal relationship of the feet.

Fifth

In the *fifth* position (closed toe-to-heel), the front heel is next to the toe of the back foot, and the feet are touching.

Following are four modifications of the first position:

Full turnout

The *full turnout* modification requires turnout in the hip sockets so that the toes point directly to the sides of the body.

Parallel

In the *parallel* version, the legs are not turned out or in, and the toes point forward. The feet may be touching or slightly separated. Some teachers prefer that the legs be slightly separated so that the hip sockets and the bones of the legs are in a more natural alignment.

Diagonal-in

In the *diagonal-in* modification, the legs are turned in from the hip sockets so that the toes point on diagonal lines inward (this position is occasionally used in modern dance).

Body Positions   For purposes of analysis, the following definitions hold. The definitions use the basic foot positions as reference points. As the illustrations show, the definitions include various body lines as well as movements in a stationary position.

In the *first* position, the feet and legs are together.

Standing   Sitting   Bending

In the *second* position, the feet and legs are apart to the side.

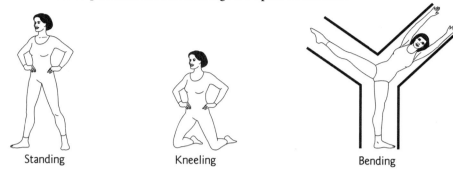

Standing   Kneeling   Bending

In the *fourth* position, the feet and legs are apart, one foot to the front and the other to the back.

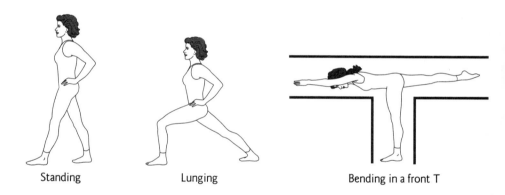

Standing   Lunging   Bending in a front T

In the third or fifth position, the legs and feet cross one another in some manner (the third and fifth positions are combined here because the placement of the feet is so similar).

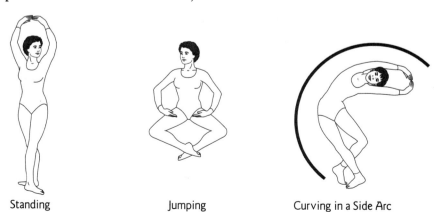

Standing   Jumping   Curving in a Side Arc

Arm Positions   Because the arm is more flexible than other parts of the body, more movement possibilities exist. Not all teachers will agree with the analysis below. Other basic arm positions may be defined. The descriptions and illustrations are presented here only as a guide to analysis. The following illustrations show curved arms.

In the *first* position, the arms are down at the sides of the body (down).

In the *second* position, the arms are raised to the sides of the body in a horizontal plane (side).

One arm is raised to the side, and the other arm is to the front—high or middle or low—in the *third* position (front-side).

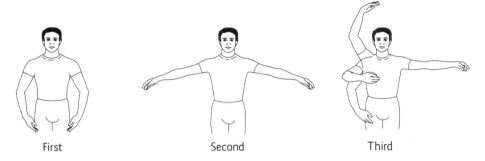

First   Second   Third

The arms are in front of the body but not on the same level in the *fourth* position (front—different levels).

In the *fifth* position, the arms are in front of the body and are on the same level (front—same levels).

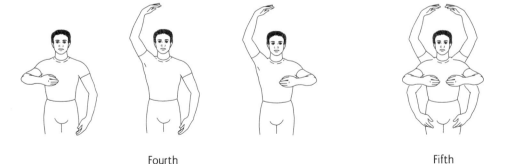

Fourth   Fifth

Examples of some variations of these arm positions follow. (With bending in the torso or rotations in the shoulder sockets, the positions also can be approximated behind the back.) These illustrations show angular arm positions, that is, the arms at sharp angles instead of gently rounded as in the previous illustration. Here the upper arm determines the basic direction.

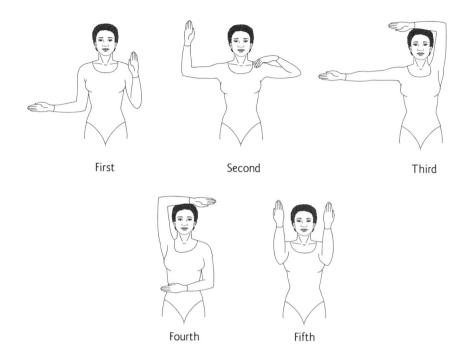

First   Second   Third

Fourth   Fifth

You might want to experiment, using the basic positions as a guide, to see how many variations you can discover by rotating the arms in the sockets, by changing the directions and levels of the arms, and by changing the degree of bend in the elbows.

In watching classroom demonstrations, ask the same sorts of questions that were applied to the analysis of movements in a stationary position: Are the arms straight or bent? In what direction? What is the angle of bend? Are the arms rotated inward or outward? Is the basic line curved or angular?

FOURTH ANALYSIS

Movement   Dance is, of course, more than static positions in space. Some schools simplify the analysis of movement by dividing it into two categories: *nonlocomotor movement,* which means movement around your own axis above a stationary support, and *locomotor movement,* which means movement through space to get yourself from one place to another.

In our analysis of basic movements in a stationary position—bending, rotating, shifting, and going to various support positions—we described nonlocomotor movements. However, these movements can also be done while you are moving from one place to another. Similarly, you can do many of the movements described below either while traveling in space or while remaining in one place.

Various kinds of movement analyses follow. If you imagine these kinds of movements combined into a movement sequence, you can begin to appreciate the interrelationship of your body and the space through which it moves. How the movement is done (quality or dynamics) and why the movement is done (motivation) provide infinite variations.

Descending or Rising Movement   Your body can descend toward the floor, as in a deep knee bend, or rise away from the floor, as in a jump. The individual parts of your body also can move toward or away from the floor. Falls and recovery are another common form of descending and rising. There are two basic kinds of falls. In one you momentarily fall off balance and then quickly reestablish your equilibrium or control. Body swings from side to side are an example. In the second you go with the natural momentum of the action until it has come to rest or until it rebounds (recovers) in another direction. For example, you fall to the floor and then rise again. Both movements are controlled partly by gravity and partly by the will of the dancer. Falls, or dropping and recovering, can be done with the whole body or with only a part of it.

Directions of Movement   The various parts of the body can move up-down, forward-backward, sideward away from or across the body, or in diagonals between front-side and back-side. And of course the whole body also can move front-back, side left or right, up-down, or on the diagonal.

An outward movement is any kind of movement that goes away from your body, as in a leg kick to the front. An inward movement is any kind of movement that comes toward the center of your body, as when you pull your outstretched arms toward your chest.

Far and Near Movements   Gestures of the arms and legs can take place away from your body so that the emphasis may be spatially oriented. When the gestures of arms and legs take place near your body, the emphasis may be more body-oriented.

Curved and Straight Paths   The whole body or a part of the body can move through space in a curved line, that is, an arclike movement. For example, if you swing your arm in a large circle, the finger tips are tracing a circular path in space. The illustration indicates another curved pattern.

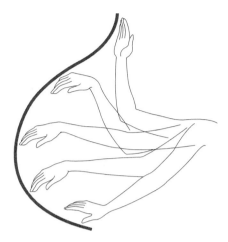

Movements can emphasize a straight line in space (spokelike) by moving toward or away from the body, or by tracing a line from one point in space to another, as shown in the illustration.

Turns There are four kinds of turns: (1) You can twist or rotate *part of your body* on its central axis. (2) You can turn *your whole body* around by revolving to the right or left around your own central axis. There are many ways such turns can be done, for example, on your own axis on both feet, on one foot, from one foot to the other foot, or while jumping. (3) You can turn in a *traveling pattern,* for example, by walking in a circle around a chair or by doing a series of turns while traveling in a straight line. (4) The whole body (or certain parts of it) can turn, as in a somersault or cartwheel revolution or as in nodding or shaking the head. Performing various turns when sitting, lying, or supported on parts of the body other than the feet expands movement possibilities.

Locomotor Movements   Movement of the entire body in some direction through space is called *traveling*. There are many ways of traveling, and they employ the other movement patterns. The following movements could be done in place as well as traveling: (1) *walk,* (2) *run,* (3) *jump*. Jumps can be analyzed in terms of whether the jump starts from one foot or both feet and lands on one foot or both feet. There are five possibilities: from both feet to both feet, from one foot to the other foot, from one foot to the same foot, from one foot to both feet, and from both feet to one foot. The Labanotation system of analysis defines these movements, respectively, as jump, leap, hop, assemblé, and sissonne.

   Whether or not these specific terms are used, recognizing the kind of preparation and landing for a jump can help you see and learn movement sequences more quickly. If you recognize, for example, that a jump starts from two feet and lands on two feet, you can quickly begin to look for other details, such as the rotation of the legs, whether the legs are straight or bent, whether the feet are pointed or flexed, and so forth.

   The visual results of the walk, run, and jump will be changed by whether or not use of the legs is stressed or unstressed, whether or not there is greater or lesser use of energy to travel upward or outward through space, and the direction in which the movement travels.

Variations   Descriptions of movements sometimes used in modern dance follow. Some can be done in place, turning, or traveling. (1) *Skip* by doing a step and a hop, alternating from one foot to the other, always with uneven rhythm. The skip might also start with the hop followed by the step. (2) *Step-hop* by stepping on one foot and hopping on the same foot. The rhythm, which is usually even, may be performed even or uneven. (3) The terms *gallop,* or *slip step,* and *slide* are open to individual interpretation. Follow the interpretation of your teacher if these actions are used in the classroom. For purposes of analysis only, slide by sliding the front foot forward, transferring the weight to the front foot; then slide the back foot toward the front foot, placing the weight onto the back foot with a "cutting action" that forces the front foot to lift quickly but with very little rise and fall of the body. The gallop, or slip step, is similar to the slide except that there is a jump into the air as the weight is transferred from one foot to the other. Children demonstrate similar action when they ride an imaginary galloping horse. (4) *Prance* like a trotting horse by stepping alternately on each foot and lifting the free leg with the knee bent. (5) A *triplet* is made up of three steps on alternating feet. The knee is bent slightly on the first step, but the legs are straight on the next two steps, and the steps are on the balls of the feet. The body moves *down, up, up, down, up, up* as the knee is bent alternately on one leg and then the other. In music, a triplet is three notes that equal one quarter note. Some teachers teach the dance triplet the same way. Others treat the triplet as three steps done to three beats in the music—in other words, a waltz. (6) *Swings* can be done with individual parts of the body or with the whole body. Swings have the quality or action of the pendulum on a clock as it traces an arclike path between two points—rising, falling, rising. The rising action is increasingly sustained, and the falling action is increasingly quickened.

Body and Spatial Designs   The body, either at rest or moving, creates a form or shape in space. The body as a whole creates one kind of shape, and the spaces around the body create another kind. These shapes may be seen as straight or curved lines and are altered by the changing relationships of the body parts to one another. In symmetrical design, the body parts are equally proportioned in the space; in asymmetrical design, the body parts are not equally proportioned. The two illustrations below indicate symmetry-asymmetry and the primary-secondary design of the body and the space around it.

A second kind of spatial design can be seen by movement in opposite directions, that is, either forward-backward, sideward out–sideward across, or up-down. The direction of the movement changes the general movement shape, which can be perceived, respectively, as advancing-retreating, widening-narrowing, and rising-sinking. The illustration at the top of page 36 suggests the movement shape of advancing-retreating.

A third kind of spatial or body design is the adaptation of the body to objects or to another person. In dance, this kind of adaptation, or sculpting of space, is often done without the presence of an actual object. The following illustration shows body adaptation in partner work.

FIFTH ANALYSIS

Qualities or Dynamics　All movement patterns take on a different look when you change their qualities or dynamics. If a pattern fails to convey some quality, it becomes devoid of any human association, and it will have little appeal to a general audience.

Qualities are related to the science of *dynamics*, which concerns the motion of bodies and the motivating forces. Dynamics is related to the greater or lesser use of energy by your body while moving in time and space. The movement may be motivated by the need to express some kind of emotional or physical state. You can use a number of basic qualities to add "shading" to your movement in the same way a painter uses contrasts in colors and shapes to enrich a painting.

The inner motivation for the movement is elusive, but the external movement can be analyzed. For purposes of analysis only, we have divided the qualities or dynamics into the four efforts conceptualized by Rudolf von Laban and F. C. Lawrence: *time, flow, weight,* and *space.* For each, the degree of effort used can be any point between two extremes. It is the mover's attitude toward a particular effort that determines how that person moves. In life the kind of movement quality or effort used is in a state of flux, adapting to the internal or external needs of the moment. In dance the dancer can consciously concentrate on changing the effort quality or qualities to add texture or shading to the movement, thereby enriching a sequence of movements.

Time   Movement may be sustained or sudden. Sustained movement can be thought of as leisurely, indulging in the use of time. Sudden movement or a series of quick motions conveys a sense of urgency.

Flow   Movement tension may be free or bound. Free flow can be thought of as unrestricted, not holding back. Bound flow can be thought of as restricted, holding back. (No negative connotation is intended by the term *bound.*)

Weight   Weight may be light or strong. Light weight can be thought of as delicate and rarified, overcoming the pull of gravity. Strong weight can be thought of as forcefully increasing the pressure or push as the body follows the pull of gravity. (Strong weight is not synonymous with the heaviness of a person or an object.)

Space   Spatial attention may be indirect or direct. Indirect spatial attention is characterized as flexible, with many overlapping foci or many shifts of attention. Direct spatial attention is channeled into a single spatial focus. Again, it is an inner attitude toward the space, so eye contact or movement of the body may not necessarily reinforce indirect or direct attention.

Movement Exercises for Dynamics   Some movement experiments may help you sense these efforts. Suppose you were given the following movement assignments. How would you move? Do these assignments influence your attitude toward the effort quality in some way?

Time   (Sustained) Lie down on the floor and stand up as slowly as you can. (Sudden) Lie down and stand up as quickly as you can.

Flow   (Free) With as little tension as possible, move about the room, freely swinging your upper body and arms. (Bound) Start to increase the tension or restrict the freedom of the movement until it feels as if you are fighting to hold back the movement.

Weight   (Light) Starting curled up on the floor, unfold your body as if it were a balloon being filled with helium; let the action float you up to a standing position. (Strong) Reverse the previous action, moving from standing to curling. Get behind your weight and strongly push it downward as you lower yourself to the floor.

Space   (Indirect) Move to different places in the room, rapidly changing your focus and direction. (Direct) Focus all of your attention on one place in the room and move to it directly.

All teachers are unique and have their own terms to help you understand dynamic forces and how the same movement changes when the quality is changed. Some teachers use word imagery or a descriptive phrase that suggests the quality. Examples include *sustained,* prolonging the movement; *vibratory,* shaking or trembling; *percussive,* beating or striking; *suspension,* a moment when the movement is lifted and held; and so forth. Try to sense in your body the quality described and how it can alter the movement.

Emphasis in a Movement Phrase

A dance movement phrase usually has a unity or logical coherence that creates a sense of harmony or completeness, which in turn leads into the next phrase. One could think of it as a movement statement with a beginning, a development, and a transition that leads into the next statement. The next statement might be a development of the original phrase or an independent new movement statement. When music (or sound) accompanies the movement, the dance phrase may or may not accompany the musical phrase. Learning to recognize and re-create the ebb and flow of your teacher's or your own movements will bring you nearer to the goal of being able to express yourself through movement.

Following are some general ideas that might aid you in analyzing what the movement phrases are about and where they are going:

1. How does the sequence start—that is, what is the first movement?
2. What is the tempo, or rate of speed?
3. Does the movement have a sense of freedom or of being held back?
4. Is there a sense of lightness, free of gravity, or does the movement suggest getting behind your weight and directing it somewhere?

5. Does the movement appear spatially focused or diffused?

6. Are the movements confined or limited to use of the space around your body, or do they use a great deal of space around the room?

7. Does the sequence of movement flow harmoniously, or is it disjointed?

8. Is the shape of the body usually symmetrical (balanced proportion of design) or asymmetrical (unbalanced proportion of design)?

9. Do the gestures and movement tend to be curved (arclike) or linear (spokelike)?

10. Is a movement accented with more force in a direction upward, downward, inward, or outward?

11. Does any movement seem to be an impulse (impelling force) leading into another movement?

12. Is there any repetitive or stressed directional movement pattern, floor pattern, or rhythmic pattern?

13. What seem to be the distinctive elements that are emphasized in the movement—rhythm, body form, line, floor pattern, or something else?

14. Can you rhythmically verbalize descriptive words that match the movement sequence, for example, slow-fast-fast-slow, up-down-out, sharp-smooth-sharp-sharp, push-pull-slash, step-step-hop, and so forth?

15. Is a characteristic manner or expression important to the movement?

16. Is there a motive or a central theme that unifies the movement?

Whether or not you follow or use these kinds of dynamic analyses is not important. Modern dance grows by the diversity of approaches. What is important is developing your ability to see others' use of dynamics and to sense your own. This ability can help you learn a movement phrase—how it starts, how it develops, how it concludes, and how it makes the transition to the next phrase. By learning movement sequences dynamically, you can avoid the possibility of learning a series of disconnected steps and postures without the inherent motivating and unifying spirit. An appreciation of dynamics also allows you to begin to understand and find your own way of moving and how movement can be used for self-expression through dance—an important element of modern dance.

SIXTH ANALYSIS

Floor Patterns   Basically, floor patterns are made up of curves, straight lines, or combinations of both. Patterns may be more intricate than the paths of movement described above. Some of the basic patterns are shown below. As a means of movement exploration, try applying these basic floor patterns to movement patterns or to stationary positions of the body. (All can be done with either the whole body or parts of the body.) The arrow indicates the direction of travel, and the square represents the performance area.

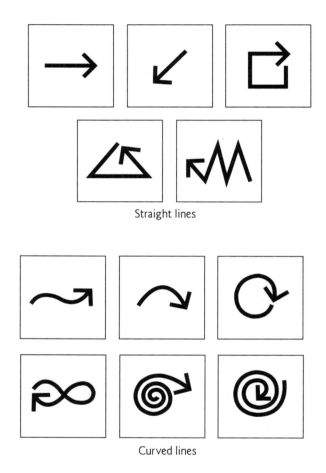

Straight lines

Curved lines

The six sets of analyses in this chapter are offered to help you more quickly learn to dance by using your mind as well as your body. Your teacher will stress some of these ideas and reject others. All approaches are valid if they help you reach your goal as a dancer.

Chapter 4
Anatomy, Injuries, and Diet

Frequently the most talented people are those most
aware of their own deficiencies and most willing
to work hard to overcome them.

LEE STRASBERG

Penrod Plastino Movement Theater, "Sonata for 2." Photo by Donald Bradburn.

BASIC ANATOMY

It is to your advantage to be familiar with the terms your teacher uses when referring to anatomy. There are correct and incorrect ways to work your body to receive the maximum results from your effort. If you know what part of the body your teacher is talking about, you can immediately apply your anatomical knowledge to the correct execution of the exercise.

We present here only the basic anatomical facts and physiological principles from which to work. If you are interested in a more thorough study, see the excellent references listed in the selected readings.

In a single dance exercise, almost every muscle in the body is used. In Table 4.1, we have indicated only the large, main groups of muscles and their common functions and movements. You can dance without knowing about these muscles, but a brief introduction to them should help you understand dance movement better.

TYPES OF INJURIES

Muscle Soreness   A vigorous dance class after a period of inactivity may cause muscle soreness, with the most common pain resulting from beginning dance classes. Such pain is referred to as acute soreness and will subside shortly after exercise ceases. Delayed soreness is another type of muscle soreness that occurs within twenty-four to forty-eight hours after exercise. This soreness, which can be severe, often increases in intensity for two to three days and then gradually subsides within seven days. A complete warm-up before dance class and a careful cool-down after class will help prevent this discomfort. A hot bath or shower may reduce muscle tension. Massage can aid the process of transmitting nutrients to the muscles; therefore, massage can relieve muscle tension, edema, and soreness.

Pain from Injuries   Pain resulting from an injury is an entirely different feeling, and proper care of the injured part must be administered in order to prevent possible permanent damage. For the most part, an injury occurs when a part of your body is weak and/or when you are tired either physically, psychologically, or both. In any class, if you are in good condition and if you work correctly, injuries should rarely occur.

Cramp   A common pain is the cramp. A cramp is an overfatigue of a muscle and may be caused by a depletion of electrolytes in the diet. It usually occurs in the arch of the foot or the calf of the leg. The pain occurs because the muscle goes into a maximum contraction involuntarily. To relieve a cramp, try to stretch the cramped part very gently or massage it in order to get a fresh blood supply to it. Generally, no permanent damage results from a cramp, but the muscle may be sore. Usually you may continue dancing as soon as severe pain subsides.

Skeletal Injuries   We can discuss only a few of the more prevalent skeletal injuries that dancers experience. General care of such injuries must include rest, ice, compression, and elevation (RICE). Ice or cold compresses must be applied immediately after an injury. This helps reduce the swelling, thereby reducing pain. You must inform your teacher as soon as any type of injury occurs. Any *major* injury must be seen by a health professional as soon as possible. This may be the school nurse, the athletic or dance trainer, or a physician. You or a friend should not try to diagnose your injury. It is hoped that dancers have access to the athletic trainer for help with injuries, as he or she is a part of the staff in most high schools and institutions of higher education.

Sprain   A sprain occurs when a joint goes beyond its normal range of movement and ligaments are damaged. This injury does not heal easily and demands a doctor's care. Ligaments and capsules in the hip and shoulder may be injured in this manner, but more commonly the injury takes place in the ligaments of the ankle. It is imperative that ice or cold compresses be applied to the area until a doctor can be consulted.

To prevent a sprained ankle, it is extremely important that the knee be centered over the ankle at all times, especially when landing from a jump or leap. If you are prone to a sprain in any part of your body, consult your doctor or teacher for exercises to strengthen that part.

Strain   A strain is usually caused by inadequate warm-up or poor flexibility. It usually occurs in the quadriceps (front of thigh) or hamstring (back of thigh). This pain can be relieved by ice and rest. Strains rarely result from taking just one class.

Shin Splint   A more serious injury is the shin splint, which afflicts the muscles on the front of the tibia (shinbone). The name *shin splint* is given to a myriad of complicated injuries to the lower leg that demand the care of a health professional. Extreme severity of this syndrome can lead to stress fractures, so it is imperative that the dancer be treated immediately when symptoms appear. Shin splint injuries are characterized by pain and irritation on the front of the lower leg. Ice, rest, and working on a stretch board sometimes help relieve these symptoms.

TABLE 4.1   Movements and Functions of Main Muscle Groups

Parts of Body	Main Muscles	Approximate Location	Main Movement
	Triceps	Bottom of upper arm (when arm is lifted to side at right angle to body with palm up)	Straightens or extends elbow
	Biceps	Top of upper arm (when arm is lifted to side at right angle to body with palm up)	Bends or flexes elbow
	Pectorals	Front of chest	Bring arm across chest, lower arm when overhead
	Trapezius and latissimus dorsi	Upper back Middle back	1. Move scapulae 2. Pull arms downward, backward, and inward
	Obliques	Over ribs on either side	Twist upper body to either side
	Rectus abdominis	From upper ribs to top of pubic bone, covering abdominal area	Raises upper body forward as in sit-up
	Quadratus lumborum	Small of back	1. Bends upper body to side 2. Stabilizes pelvis and spine
	Iliopsoas	Lumbar spine to femur	1. Strong hip flexor 2. Raises the thigh to the trunk *or* flexes the trunk to the thighs against resistance
	Gluteals	Buttocks	1. Stabilize hip 2. Extend hip
	Quadriceps	Front of thigh	Extends leg in forward movements
	Hamstrings	Back of upper leg	1. Bend knee 2. Extend hip
	Gastrocnemius (gastrox or calf)	Back of lower leg	1. Points foot 2. Raises leg to ball of foot (half toe) 3. Bends knee
	Tibialis anterior	Front of lower leg	Flexes the foot (dorsiflexion)
	Tibialis posterior and peroneals	Around either side of ankle	All muscles contribute to move ankle in circle
	Achilles tendon	Lower part of leg and heel on back of leg; longer part of gastrox (calf) muscle	Same as gastrox

Common Exercise and/or Weight-Training Suggestion	Significance for Dance	Discussion
Push-up Weights: standing triceps extension; hold weight in both hands overhead, let weight drop to neck level and to the back and up again	1. Strengthens arms for falls and lifts 2. Gives firmness under the arm	Development imperative for control of back and upper arm strength
Push-up and pull-up Weights: curls (bending the lower arm to the upper arm while holding weight)	Strengthens arms for falls and lifts	Generally very weak in women; both men and women need this strength for control
Push-up Weights: Bench press, dumbbell fly, and pullover	1. Provides firm chest muscles 2. Needed for lifts and falls	Strength needed for development of chest
Push-up, pull-up, chin-ups Weights: with arms extended wide apart overhead, pull weight down to neck level and push back up	Gives control of entire back and arms	Development of entire back for control in balancing off center turns and body control in general
Twist or rotate upper body	Makes small, strong waist	Vulnerable in lifts; can be strained
Sit-up: with knees bent and legs at 90°, crunch or raise only upper body toward knees	Keeps abdomen flat if done regularly	Strength of this area increased by twisting movements during sit-up
1. Bend upper body to side 2. Sit-up as described above	Contributes to strong lower back	*Injury*—General weakness Sit-ups and stretches of the back imperative
Stretch the thigh to the back while maintaining the integrity of the hip	Can contribute to lordosis or sway back	Must be stretched constantly
1. Turn out the leg from hip socket 2. Lift leg to back 3. Weights: leg press	Contributes to thigh turnout	Must be developed in males especially for strength in leaps and jumps
1. Lift leg forward 2. Straighten leg at knee joint 3. Pull up kneecap 4. Weights: quadriceps press	1. Steadies knee joint 2. Straightens knee 3. Provides stability for knee joint	*Injury*—Strain At onset of pain, apply ice, rest until pain stops, do easy movements
1. Touch toes with fingers without bending knees 2. Sit erect on floor with legs extended straight forward 3. Weights	1. Bends knee 2. Must be stretched constantly and also strengthened	*Injury*—Strain At onset of pain apply ice; rest until pain stops, no stretching until no pain
1. Jump 2. While holding weight, rise up and down on a raised surface so heel drops below surface	1. Tires easily 2. Strain muscle in jump 3. Points ankle and foot (plantar flex)	*Injury*—Temporary soreness from sudden overuse and strains *Prevention*—Should be strengthened and stretched
Overuse common Do toe pulls with towel	Flexes foot and ankle	Major part of shin-splint syndrome. Ice, stretchboard needed
1. Rotate ankle in circle 2. Raise and lower on stair or board	1. Helps protect Achilles tendon 2. Supports ankle in all foot movements	*Injury*—Sprained ankle *Prevention*—Keep ankle in line with center of knee
Jump Weights: calf machine	1. Must be stretched constantly 2. Thickest and strongest tendon in body	*Injury*—Tears apart by violent overstretching *Prevention*—When coming down from a jump, land on ball of foot, lower heel to floor, bend leg

Many other kinds of injuries could occur in a dance class, but if you work properly, injuries should not occur.

INJURY PREVENTION AND RECUPERATION

The training of a modern dancer has continued to change since modern dance as an art form began some ninety years ago. Current training methods reflect the increasing demands of more difficult techniques and higher performance standards. Although these rigorous criteria have produced more injuries, both health professionals and dance teachers are now more conscious of how to care for dancers so that injuries don't occur. Only recently has the public become aware of the injuries faced by dancers and of the fact that a dancer is one of the finest trained athletes.

A ten-year study by the Dance Medicine Group at the authors' university (University of California, Irvine) on the physical screening and follow-up of 500 student dancers has shown that the majority of injuries in student dancers occur from the hip down. This same incidence has also been reported in the literature on professional dancers.

Although a dancer can sustain a sudden sprain, strain, or break, the most common injury develops over a period of time through overuse. The continual repetition of the same movements causes most of the injuries in dance. High-level student and professional dancers experience these overuse injuries more often than do beginning or intermediate student dancers, because professionals dance at least eight hours a day six days a week.

Your schedule as a beginning or intermediate student usually includes one or two dance classes a day and perhaps two or three additional hours a week in rehearsal. Performances are usually scattered throughout the year. This schedule should not produce injuries that keep you from dancing, but it may produce problems in your body similar to those the professionals have, because you also perform the same kinds of movement over and over again.

Most of the injuries you will incur involve the soft tissues: muscles, tendons, ligaments, and bursae. These are acute injuries, which means that you must rest the area of the body that hurts. To stay in shape during your recuperation, you should do other types of exercise that do not involve the injured part.

Exercise   We recommend several forms of exercise to increase your strength and endurance both when you are healthy and dancing and when you are recuperating from an injury. An additional problem with any injury is the possibility of its recurrence. This is why alternate and additional forms of conditioning such as weight training, warming up, and cooling down are so important to the continued health of the dancer. There are other ways to condition the body—including Pilates-based, Alexander, and Feldenkrais techniques, low-impact aerobic exercise designed especially for the dancer, water exercises, and stationary bicycling—but they are too detailed to include in this book. Any additional conditioning program *must* be discussed with and approved by your teacher so that the extra work enhances your performance and does not damage it.

Weight Training   We have chosen to discuss weight training as a form of additional conditioning for dancers for two reasons: (1) It is the most readily available form of conditioning, since most schools and all private health clubs have the equipment, and (2) the authors have had remarkable positive results from the weight-training program in their own department over the past five years. Weight training for female dancers must be accomplished with low weight and high repetition to build strength without bulk. A female dancer should use a sufficient amount of weight to stress the muscle but not so heavy a weight as to fatigue the muscle and cause unwanted bulk. It is important to train both the lower and the upper body and to perform all the movements through a full range of motion. Dancers will not lose flexibility when lifting weights if they warm up before lifting and continue to take their regular dance classes. Male dancers need to do the more traditional weight-training protocol that particularly develops the upper body and also includes work on the lower body. We recommend that both male and female dancers lift weights three times a week.

No one should begin to lift weights without instruction from a weight-training coach; most educational institutions have such an expert on staff who will provide the necessary instruction. As an incentive to start a weight-training program, you should know that almost all Russian male ballet dancers lift weights and that the women and men in many modern-dance companies in the United States participate in conditioning exercises, including weight lifting.

Proper Body Alignment   Prevention of injury is best accomplished through correct alignment and proper working in class, rehearsal, performance, and the off-season, which is often the summer months for students. Many of the injuries that do occur in dancers can be directly related to faulty technique and incorrect placement of the body. We discussed basic alignment in Chapter 3; we now show the placement of the body as viewed from the side with the plumb line in order to reinforce the importance of proper body alignment. It is, of course, even more important that the body be properly placed when moving in dance. Your teacher is the expert who can tell you when you are "out of alignment." Some of the more prevalent alignment problems that may cause later injuries include hyperextended knees (swaybacked knees), lordosis of back (swayback), pronation of feet (roll-in), supination of feet (roll-out), and knock-knees. You should be aware of these basic common discrepancies in body alignment so that you can avoid or correct them.

The Dancer's Posture

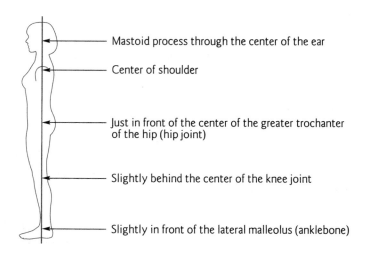

Mastoid process through the center of the ear

Center of shoulder

Just in front of the center of the greater trochanter of the hip (hip joint)

Slightly behind the center of the knee joint

Slightly in front of the lateral malleolus (anklebone)

Dancers are slightly more forward in their posture than nondancers, because they must be ready to rise to their toes or to move quickly and in any direction at any moment.

Warm-up and Cool-down   Warm-up serves two main functions for dancers: (1) It brings focus to the body and the mind for the important work ahead, and (2) it prepares the physical instrument to perform those functions by raising the core temperature of the body. Every dance class must be preceded by a warm-up period. A general warm-up should last from eight to ten minutes and engage the major joints and muscles. The warm-up should start slowly and gradually add increasingly difficult movement. Advanced range of motion should be increased only after the joints are pliable and the body is sweating. Research has shown that the warm-up should occur no more than fifteen minutes before a performance. Cool-down is as important as warm-up and must occur after every class and performance. This is the time to let the heart rate return to normal (about 100 beats per minute), do stretching exercises, and let sweating subside. Usually, five to ten minutes after a class is adequate time for the body to cool down. Fewer injuries seem to occur in those dancers who warm up and cool down.

Proper Rest   Getting proper rest is one of the most important ways to prevent injuries. Many times, injuries occur because the dancer is exhausted either physically or psychologically, or both. You probably will be working or going to school full-time in addition to studying dance. With this double burden, you must establish your priorities in a way that enables you to rest and to get the sleep you need.

DIET AND FITNESS

Modern dance should not produce the bulky muscles familiar to a football player or a wrestler. These sport activities warrant the development of heavy muscles for strength. As a dancer you need long, lean lines so that the clarity of the movement is not obscured. You need minimum weight so that you can perform intricate movements easily.

You as a dancer must convey the ideal physique or figure. No one has a perfect body! But by proper dance training and a proper balance of exercise, rest, and diet, you can more quickly achieve the illusion of the ideal.

Dancers are notoriously abusive of their bodies. They often expect their bodies to respond instantly and perfectly on command without having given them proper care. You cannot expect to deal with the great physical demands made on your body without properly caring for it.

The word *diet* often suggests hunger, regimented eating, or eating only certain kinds of food for extended periods. To the dancer, diet should signify temperance in living habits.

As a dancer, you cannot afford extra calories in foods that do not make an appreciable contribution to your body. Even if you are of a good weight, size, and structure to be a dancer, it is to your advantage to evaluate your daily intake of food.

The current dietary recommendation for active teenagers and young adults is to choose foods from all food groups, following the 3-4-4-2 dietary plan each day; this translates to 3 servings from milk and milk products, 4 from vegetables and fruits, 4 from grain products, and 2 from meats and meat alternatives. Athletes often follow a different dietary plan, which combines the meat and dairy groups to compose one group of foods. They consume the bulk of their diet from the vegetable/fruit and grain groups. The ideal dietary plan for dancers is 60 to 70 percent complex carbohydrates (sugars and starches), 15 to 20 percent fat, and 15 to 20 percent protein to produce abundant energy.

Either dietary plan can work for you. The key fact to remember is

that one gram of fat contains nine calories, whereas one gram of carbo-
hydrate or protein contains four calories. You can, therefore, eat more
carbohydrates or protein and consume fewer calories than you would
with the same amount of fat.

To explain the physiology of the energy cycle in simple terms, we
begin with complex carbohydrates, which are stored in the body as glycogen. Glycogen is broken down into glucose, which is the main fuel for mus-
cular activity. Glycogen is not easily stored in the body; this is why
carbohydrates must be continually replenished. Dancers do not use as
much energy as do endurance athletes, so they usually need fewer calories.

The importance of a balanced diet during the adolescent and young
adult years cannot be overemphasized, especially for active dancers. Adequate vitamins, minerals, and calories must be consumed to keep you
healthy now and to prepare your body for the later years. Female dancers
need to be especially concerned with consuming adequate calcium (nonfat milk and milk products, tofu, greens, legumes) and iron (red meat,
eggs, green vegetables, legumes). Vitamin and mineral tablets have sometimes been recommended to supplement this part of the diet. Supple-
ments must be taken in conjunction with the proper foods in order to
be fully beneficial. Taking them is not recommended unless you are
directed to do so by a physician or registered dietitian.

If you want to lose weight, you should be able to do so on 1,300 to
1,500 calories a day (we do not recommend fewer calories than this),
especially if you are taking dance classes at the same time. If you do not
lose weight, you may have a medical problem. See your physician if this
situation occurs.

The reduction of fat in your diet and the addition of carbohydrates
will help you lose weight and hopefully gain more energy. Fat comes
mostly from butter, whole milk, cream, untrimmed meats, and the unsat-
urated vegetable oils that are in margarine and most foods stored on the
grocery shelf. Lean beef, skinless poultry, and fish are almost entirely protein, and complex carbohydrates come from whole-grain cereals and
breads, pastas, fruits, and vegetables. Of course, several foods, such as
legumes (peas and beans), have both protein and carbohydrates.

Here are some ways for dancers to lose or maintain weight:

1. "Grazing" (eating several small meals daily) is an especially effective
   eating regimen to accommodate the intermittent schedules of students and performers.

2. Coffee, tea, and diet colas have zero calories, but the caffeine in these
   drinks dehydrates and stimulates the body when your body is actu-
   ally in need of rehydration (fluid). Water is the best fluid for all
   dancers. Try to drink eight glasses of water every day.

3. Eat fruit, raw vegetables, and air-popped popcorn in place of cookies, chips, and salty snack foods.

4. For dessert, eat nonfat frozen yogurt; one cup has only 144 calories, compared to 349 calories for one cup of ice cream.

5. Participate in an aerobic activity for thirty minutes three times a week. This includes swimming laps, running, taking fitness classes, riding a bicycle, using a treadmill, or engaging in other physical activities.

6. Establish a reasonable weight-loss goal of no more than one pound a week, and do not weigh in more than once a week. Remember that it takes a long time to gain weight, and it takes the same amount of time to lose it. Try to be reasonable.

The preoccupation with abnormal thinness that now permeates our society has produced an alarming number of sufferers from eating disorders. These disorders are not limited to professional and student dancers; it is now believed that more than 20 percent of young women suffer from more than at least one of the symptoms of an eating disorder. But we do know that the extreme thinness expected of dancers, gymnasts, models, and some other female athletes has made eating disorders a reality in these groups as well as among male wrestlers and jockeys, who must "make weight," and male divers and models, who also rely on the "look of the body to perform the skill."

There are two types of eating disorders: *anorexia nervosa,* or self-starvation, and *bulimia,* a related syndrome involving binge eating followed by vomiting, laxative abuse, use of diuretics, or fasting. Both disorders can be fatal if carried to extremes, so it is very important for a person who suffers from either of these disorders to seek help as soon as possible. Some of the symptoms of eating disorders are low self-esteem, guilt when eating high-calorie food, obsessive preoccupation with weight, and unrealistically high goals and expectations of oneself. Often another dancer or a friend can identify the problem before the teacher becomes aware of the situation. It is important that you talk to your teacher confidentially about the possibility of you or anyone you know having an eating disorder.

Avoiding injuries, maintaining leanness, and giving maximum energy are the major concerns for dancers. Understanding the body and how it functions contributes to the essence of a dancer's existence.

Chapter 5
History

For last year's words belong to last year's language
And next year's words await another voice.

T. S. ELIOT

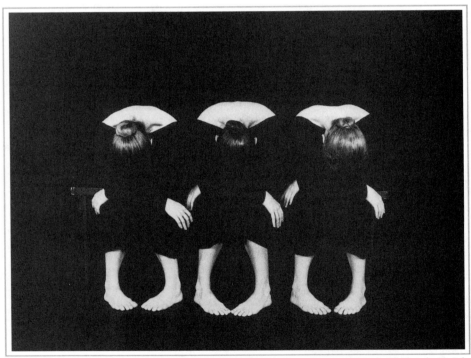

Lewitzky Dance Company, "Episode #1." Photo by Vic Luke.

The dance discussed in this book has been developed in the last hundred years. It was called "modern" because it broke from the traditions and disciplines of the stiff formality of the ballet of the nineteenth century. At the beginning, modern dance was a way of life, an expression of the freedom of the spirit, unfettered by outdated traditions and worn-out beliefs. Modern dance was in its adolescence at the time of the women's suffrage movement, Prohibition, World War I, and new movements in art. One such movement was called expressionism. Expressionism, which originated in painting, is a subjective expression of the artist's personal reaction to events or objects through distortion, abstraction, or symbolism. It was a dominating influence on modern dance.

PIONEERS IN DANCE

Many artists late in the nineteenth century were searching for a means to express their individuality and concern for humankind. Modern dance was one of the ways some of these people sought to free their creative spirit. At the beginning, there was no exacting technique, no foundation from which to build. In later years, through trial, error, and genius, the techniques and principles of the movement were established. Eventually, innovators even drew from what they considered the dread ballet, but first they had to discard all that was academic so that the new could be discovered. Male artists, including Rudolf von Laban and Kurt Jooss (1901–1979) in Europe and Ted Shawn in the United States, helped form the beginnings of modern dance, but the dominant pioneering forces in the field were women. The beginnings of modern dance were forming before Isadora Duncan, but she was the first person to bring modern dance to general audiences and see it accepted and acclaimed.

Her search for a natural movement form sent her to nature. She believed movement should be as natural as the swaying of the trees and the rolling waves of the sea and should be in harmony with the movements of the earth. These beautiful ideals have often been misinterpreted and grossly misused in dance. Modern dance has often been thought of as young girls imitating the blooming of a flower. Contrary to popular belief, Duncan never improvised on stage and personally supervised every detail of her performances. Her great contributions are found in three areas.

First, she began the expansion of the kinds of movements that could be used in dance. Before Duncan danced, ballet was the only type of dance performed in concert. In the ballet, the feet and legs were emphasized, with virtuosity shown by complicated, codified positions and movements. Isadora performed dance by using her entire body in the freest possible way, taking her inspiration from the ancient Greeks. She did not develop a technique as we know it today. Her dance stemmed from her soul and spirit. She was one of the pioneers who broke tradition so that others might be able to develop the art.

Her second contribution was in dance costume. She discarded corsets, ballet shoes, and stiff costumes and replaced them with flowing Grecian tunics, bare feet, and unbound hair. She believed in the natural body being allowed to move freely, and her dress displayed this ideal.

Her third contribution was in the use of music. In her performances, she used the symphonies of great masters, including Beethoven and Wagner, which was not the usual custom.

She was as exciting and eccentric in her personal life as in her dance. Her two beautiful, illegitimate children who were tragically drowned, her many loves, and her death by strangulation from a long trailing scarf that accidentally wrapped around the wheel of a sports car all symbolize her dramatic life. She threw away the conventions that characterized the time in which she lived, 1878–1927. She has been portrayed in a film, *The Loves of Isadora,* and the dancing in this film is a near duplication of the way Duncan moved.

While Isadora Duncan looked to the West and classical Greece for inspiration for her new dance, Ruth St. Denis (1877–1968) looked to the East and the Orient to discover a new movement form. In 1906, she performed *Radha,* a dance that used an Oriental theme to communicate a spiritual message. It was so significant that it continued to be performed even in the 1940s, when Miss Ruth (as she was usually addressed) was in her sixties. She was interested not just in virtuosity in dance but also in communicating an idea. She did not develop a technique. Instead, she believed music was to be "visualized" in order to produce dance movements.

In the scheme of the development of modern dance, Ruth St. Denis holds a vital position. She not only made specific contributions of her own but also provided, through the Denishawn Company, a proving ground for the next generation of dancers, including Martha Graham, Doris Humphrey, and Charles Weidman. Denishawn, which was a partnership and a marriage between Miss Ruth and Ted Shawn, proved successful for some sixteen years. During these years, Denishawn was financially self-supporting—a unique position in the history of modern dance companies.

Ted Shawn (1891–1972) was codirector of Denishawn, and if Miss Ruth was its spirit, he was its form. He performed and choreographed in Denishawn until it dissolved in 1931. From 1933 to 1940, he directed a company of male dancers who were ex-athletes. He was influenced by

François Delsarte, who in the early nineteenth century had developed a technique of pantomime that honestly expressed emotion. Shawn wrote about these techniques in a book, *Every Little Movement.*

Shawn taught baseball, football, and basketball players, wrestlers, and track stars dances with strong masculine themes, such as *Olympiad* and *Labor Symphony.* Through his efforts, he helped raise the status of the male dancer in the United States by choreographing themes that promoted the masculine characteristics of the dancers.

Another major contribution by Ted Shawn to the dance world was the founding of the Jacob's Pillow center in Massachusetts. This is a residence for dancers where they may study and perform. Late each summer, a festival is held there where works are presented in concert.

Mary Wigman, who came from the German School of modern dance, was another influential pioneer. Wigman (1886–1973) was regarded as the genius and the leader of German modern dance from 1924 to 1943. She studied dance with Émile Jacques-Dalcroze (1865–1950), who created a way to teach the coordination of music and body movements called *eurythmics,* and with Rudolf von Laban (1879–1958), who developed one of the methods of recording body movements on paper, which is now called *Labanotation.*

Because she was concerned with self-expression, Wigman's contributions included psychological and emotional approaches to creativity. She felt that dance should be movement alone, so she composed dances without music. She fully explored the use of space. Her dances were described as "dark and somber . . . largely an ecstasy of gloom, stressing the demonic and macabre" (Margaret Lloyd, *The Borzoi Book of Modern Dance* [Brooklyn, N.Y.: Dance Horizons, Inc., 1949], 12).

Hanya Holm (1898–   ), Wigman's pupil, adapted the German modern dance to the needs and characteristics of American dancers. As a master teacher of modern dance, she influenced many dancers with her concepts of space. Holm was one of the few modern dance choreographers also successful as a choreographer for the Broadway musical stage. Her most famous musical was *My Fair Lady.*

Probably the most exacting technique and the greatest number of choreographic works have come from Martha Graham (1894–1991). Her technique is built on the breathing cycle of the body and its principle of "contraction and release." (Other principles developed by her are "motor memory" and "percussive movement.") In brief, Graham's dance is built on the process of inhaling and exhaling. She believes that in inhaling the body has an aerial quality of release and in exhaling the body "drive has gone down and out" in contraction. Many of today's dancers,

From top:
Ruth St. Denis,
Martha Graham,
Merce Cunningham,
Doris Humphrey, Charles Weidman

From top:
Ted Shawn,
Bella Lewitzky,
Alvin Ailey,
Isadora Duncan,
Alwin Nikolais

choreographers, and modern dance classes have been influenced by her technique.

Another major contribution by Graham has been in the area of choreography and performance. She is considered to have been one of the finest dance concert performers. She utilized the wide spectrum of life in the themes of her outstanding works. She often used themes from Greek drama to symbolize and probe humans' inner qualities. Her dance company has included some of the outstanding dancers in the world.

Martha Graham and Doris Humphrey both left Denishawn, and each established her own school. Both developed theories and philosophies of movement that are significant to the growth of modern dance, and both are considered to be in the art's third generation.

Doris Humphrey (1895–1958) was a protégée of Ruth St. Denis, and her movements were of the same lyrical quality. She built her dance principles on the "fall-recovery" theory, which she created. She believed dance movement came about by periods of unbalance and balance in the body. She stated that fall-recovery consisted of three separate movements: the *fall*, the *recovery* from the fall, and the *suspension* held at the peak of recovery. She also perfected compositions using large-scale dramatic themes for groups of dancers.

Humphrey formed an alliance with Charles Weidman (1901–1975), who had also been in the Denishawn Company and is known for his biting, satirical dance works and for his skill as a performer. Together they formed one branch of American modern dance. Humphrey performed her works until 1945, when crippling arthritis ended her performing career. She continued choreographing and working until her death.

Some of Humphrey's most brilliant works from 1945 on were created for José Limón (1908–1972), an important choreographer in his own right. His powerful body and magnificent carriage and bearing always marked his strong masculine performances. Limón formed his own company in 1946 and continued to choreograph dramatic works until his death.

Lester Horton (1906–1953) was a major modern dance teacher and choreographer who chose to work in Southern California rather than New York. His dance technique is one of the three to survive from those of the early modern dance pioneers. Graham's and Humphrey's are the other two technique forms widely taught today. Horton was known for his use of form and color, the theatricalization of ethnic dance forms, and the development and training of other significant artists of modern dance. Some of those artists include Alvin Ailey, Carmen DeLavallade, James Truitte, fashion designer Rudi Gernreich, and Bella Lewitzky.

SUCCEEDING GENERATIONS OF MODERN DANCERS

Of the dancers who worked in the 1960s, Merce Cunningham (1919–) stirred the most controversy with his works. Cunningham choreographs "by chance," holding to the idea that "any movement can follow any other movement." Regarded as avant-garde, he choreographs and performs works that audiences either adore or abhor, depending on their individual convictions. His admirers point to his fine artistic sense, his intelligence, and his superb company as factors that make the works he creates brilliant movement pieces. Cunningham maintained a long artistic collaboration with composer John Cage (1912–1992), known for his philosophy that all sound should be regarded as music. Works produced under their collaboration created new artistic realms.

Alwin Nikolais (1912–1993) was another American modern dance choreographer. His contribution was in the creation of a form of theater that includes props, costumes, films, slides, sound, and light as extensions of the bodies of the dancers. His visual effects and illusions often remind the audience of events in their own experience, yet the works contain no story or conventional plot. The dancers' bodies are often distorted or hidden in the costumes and props to emphasize Nikolais's abstract images and suggestions.

Another renowned choreographer is Anna Sokolow (1912–), whose powerful social statements characterize her works. Her commitment to the socialist movement, evident in her early works, gave way over time to a more general concern with the feelings and problems of all humanity. Sokolow has used many different types of music, including jazz, and has choreographed extensively in Mexico and Israel as well as in the United States.

Black Choreographers   Many modern dancers have contributed to the development of modern dance as an art in America. Alvin Ailey's (1931–1989) great gift was his ability to present exciting, theatrical pieces that reflect the black experience. His first company was composed of all black dancers, but now his company is composed of dancers of all races who perform works by many choreographers. Ailey's present repertory company performs works that combine art and a unique vision of dance. The company is very popular and tours regularly.

Several other black dancers have significantly influenced modern dance. Donald McKayle (1930–) is known for his use of dramatic tension and narrative to portray the black experience in his dances. One of his best-known works is *Games,* which is based on children playing in the city streets. McKayle describes his work *Rainbow Round My Shoulder* as "based on chain gangs dreaming of freedom symbolized in the shape of a woman." His most recent work, for the José Limón Dance Company, *Heartbeats,* utilizes international song and dance to illuminate the human connections.

Gus Solomons (1940–) and Garth Fagan are two other outstanding black choreographers. Solomons, who danced in the Merce Cunningham Company before starting his own company, is known for his use of architectural form in his choreography. Fagan uses a combination of strong modern-dance technique, the distinct qualities of African movement, and black culture to choreograph dances. These significant artists all bring their experience as blacks to their unique choreographic statements.

Other Choreographers of the 1960s and 1970s   Paul Taylor (1930–) also has taken modern dance to new artistic levels. Taylor danced with Graham and Cunningham but has developed a style that is definitely his own. He is known for his choreographic wit, logical placings of movements, groupings of dancers, and satire. He has also created pieces that cleverly repeat a limited number of movements over and over again in unusual ways. He has not performed since 1974, but he still choreographs for his company extensively.

Bella Lewitzky (1916–) is unique to the world of modern dance because she made her international reputation as an artist in California instead of New York. Not since Denishawn had a modern dance choreographer of major importance become established elsewhere than New York. Like Alvin Ailey, she was trained in California by Lester Horton. Her choreography is known for its powerful images and for extensive use of space, isolations, and quick movements. Lewitzky was always known for her extraordinary ability as a performing artist.

During the 1960s, modern dance reflected the social and political unrest that pervaded the decade. Many changes occurred. The only consistent characteristic was a discarding of the idea of theatricality for the use of everyday, pedestrian movement. Some dancers and choreographers were saying no to the idea of modern dance as it then existed.

Many times, traditional leotards, tights, and theatrical costumes were discarded and replaced by utilitarian garments such as overalls and hard hats, gym shorts and tennis shoes, sweat shirts and jeans—or even nudity. The 1960s and 1970s produced new names for modern dance, including antidance, nondance, minimal dance, environmental dance, dance without walls, verbal dance, and alternate space dance. Dance was sometimes performed in nontraditional spaces such as museums, malls, parking lots, parks, streets, and country clubs. Such spaces change the way dance is performed, and many times the dance is directed and choreographed by a dancer but performed by dancers and nondancers alike.

These periods of fertile creativity were characterized by a fresh look at time, space, and sound. Much of the movement was antiproscenium theater, in which ordinary movement by ordinary people in ordinary places is considered valid as art. Many dancers collaborated on an equal basis with composers and studio artists to create pieces, or "events" as they were sometimes called. Before this generation of dancers, choreographers had given ideas to a composer or designer and then waited for the results. Now the collaboration often took place simultaneously, with all the artists contributing to the work.

As the decade of the 1970s drew to a close, two distinct camps of modern dance existed. One camp became more and more technically oriented and produced dances that were more and more difficult to perform. Dancers needed to study for periods of time with a choreographer in order to develop the style and technique needed to perform that choreographer's works. These choreographers followed more directly the established artists of the generation who had preceded them. They did not necessarily create in the same way that their teachers had, but they used many of the preceding generation's methods and ideas to create their own original works. Some of the artists involved with the more theatrically motivated modern dance of the 1970s were Murray Louis, Jennifer Mueller, Bill Evans, Cliff Keuter, Twyla Tharp, Lar Lubovitch, Gloria Newman, and Pilobolus.

The other camp became more and more antidance. Time, space, and energy were altered to make new forms, meanings, and nonmeanings in the modern dance. Most of these choreographers had also studied and worked with the preceding generation of choreographers, but they discarded many of that generation's ideas to do new, different, exciting things in dance. A few of the artists involved with this camp of modern dance in the 1970s were Don Redlich, Rudy Perez, Meredith Monk, Kei Takei, and Anna Halprin.

The Judson Group and the Grand Union Group were instrumental in expanding modern dance performance to include many of these new ideas. The Judson Group was a coalition of choreographers, dancers, and other artists who worked and performed from 1962 to 1968 in the Judson Church in New York City. This collective was composed of a diversity of artists who interacted and created new ideas about a new kind of modern dance. The Judson was followed by the Grand Union from 1970 to 1976. Several of the artists belonged to both groups. Some ideas produced were the inclusion of improvisation within the performance of a dance piece, "marking" or walking through rehearsal and presenting this concept as legitimate performance, ever-developing dance pieces that would change with each performance, and the alteration of the order of sections of completed dance works each time they were performed. These and other concepts were important in the expansion of the concepts of modern dance. Some of the most important contributors to these movements were Yvonne Rainer, Steve Paxton, Douglas Dunn, and David Gordon.

In California, Anna Halprin (1920–) has been redefining modern dance since the late 1950s. Her contribution to the ever-changing and evolving nature of modern dance has influenced many dancers and artists. Her current work in AIDS and with cancer patients is an extension and evolution of her earlier work in improvisation and process. This work has set her apart as one of the major innovators in modern dance.

Trends in the 1980s   Modern dance in the 1980s was characterized by several trends. Dance technique became more difficult and specific. Some movements that might typically be associated with sports or nondance activities were incorporated into choreographed pieces and used as dance movement. One choreographer who might be defined in this way is Trisha Brown, who uses movements that seem to defy gravity. Pilobolus combines athleticism, traditional modern dance, and the support of another dancer's weight in unusual ways to produce often humorous dances. Dancers seem to defy gravity. This group creates choreography by group decision.

Another development in the eighties was the alteration of the proscenium theater stage with all types of materials, including water, peat moss, rocks, or leaves, on the stage floor. Pina Bausch (1940–) uses these materials to enhance and influence her intense, dramatic concept of modern dance. Japanese choreographer Kei Takei uses such objects to intensify and project her concept of dance. One of her continuing projects, entitled *Light,* is continually developing and evolving.

Another trend that became significant in the 1980s involves choreographers who consult with other artists in related fields to collaborate and produce works. Some of the more prominent choreographers who work in this manner are Martha Clarke, David Gordon, Lucinda Childs, and Molissa Fenley. These choreographers collaborate with set, costume, and lighting designers, music composers, video artists, and others. All of these artists work together to produce works that are based on movement but additionally incorporate ideas from theater, art, and music. Several artists are responsible for the final product, with the choreographer usually conceiving and directing the entire production. This method differs from the traditional methods of production, in which designers are often not consulted until after the choreographer has conceived and developed the work alone.

Some choreographers compose their own music as well as their own dances and are known as a choreographer/composer. One such artist, Laura Dean (1945–), has made significant contributions to modern dance through her use of spinning and repeated strong rhythmical patterns. Another choreographer/composer is Meredith Monk, who uses her own musical compositions and has recorded record albums that have been recognized by the musical establishment.

Many contemporary choreographers continually produce significant works and tour the United States and other parts of the world. The scope of this book allows for a brief discussion of only a few of these artists.

Mark Morris (1956–) has been lauded as one of the most influential choreographers for the future of modern dance. He has been critically acclaimed for his use of music, his understanding of many and varied dance forms, and his ability to create energetic, explosive and sometimes outrageous dances. He uses all sizes and shapes of male and female dancers and does not necessarily use them in the traditional male/female roles. He may even reverse their roles on stage. He maintains his own modern-dance company as well as choreographing extensively for opera and ballet companies.

Lar Lubovitch (1945–) uses movement that is defined for the human body. He considers his dancers to be more important to him than any other element in his choreography, so his dances are designed to be humanistic. The Bill T. Jones and Arnie Zane Company uses movement that often evokes startling images of playful violence, outrage, and sometimes warm, emotional gestures. Since the death of Zane in 1988, Jones (1952–) has become a seminal influence in modern dance. One of his major works, *Still/Here,* deals with the issues of AIDS, death, and living.

New Trends in the 1990s   Modern dance continues to evolve and change in the nineties because of many influences, including decreased funding from governmental agencies for arts in the United States, less appeal to dance audiences and theater patrons, an influx of major and innovative foreign dance companies, and the devastating effect of the disease AIDS on the field.

Some choreographers, for example, Twyla Tharp (1942–), have reestablished their own modern dance companies after having made innovative choreographic contributions to major ballet companies. Trisha Brown's company now performs in prestigious proscenium theaters to music by established composers. In the seventies, Brown (1936–) created mostly without music and in alternative spaces.

Many international modern-dance companies regularly tour the United States, including Pina Bausch's Tanztheater Wuppertal from Germany, Netherlands Dance Theater from Holland, France's Maguy Marin and the Lyons Opéra Ballet, and the Butoh-based Sankai Juku from Japan. These companies offer diverse views of modern dance, and all use extraordinary visual and theatrical effects with distinctive cultural viewpoints.

Several other themes dominate modern dance in the 1990s, including the use of throwing and catching of the body with gymnastic and wrestling techniques as the basis for choreographic statement. Some productions include elements from tap dancing, rhythmical percussion, and folk forms to appeal to new audiences. The shows *Stomp* and *Riverdance* show how modern dance continues to redefine itself by fusing other forms of movement with current practices to find contemporary modes of expression.

The vitality of developing modern dance is less dependent on the New York scene than in the past. In major cities, a number of dancers, choreographers, and small companies are establishing a new kind of dance based on the experience inherent to their locale. As these companies establish themselves, they are able to tour to the dance capital, New York City, and to tour internationally, bringing with them a new point of view on modern dance expression.

As dancers and choreographers explore new ways of moving and create more meaningful ways to communicate with the audience, modern dance changes, incorporates, and adopts these new ideas. The difference between the pioneers and the dancers of today is that today's dancers have a strong, proven foundation from which to work.

Modern dance of the eighties and nineties has continued in the tradition of the pioneers of the movement. It continues to change, evolve, and reflect the time in which it is created. Modern dance is influenced by societal issues, political concerns, the history of the art form, evolutions in the other arts, and the expansion and development of dance technique. Modern dance continually grows, develops, and reflects the moment of its creation and creator. This is the amazement and excitement of the art form.

Chapter 6
Improvisation

The Process is the Purpose . . . Nonseparation
of life and art.

ANNA HALPRIN

Bill T. Jones/Arnie Zane Dance Company. Photo © 1997 Johan Elbers

Creativity is important to problem solving in many disciplines, including science, business, the arts, and other areas. Creative solutions to problems significantly enrich our society and our institutions. The nurturing of the creative process is an essential part of dancers' education and an essential part of empowering their creative resources. Improvisation and choreography are two structured methods for fostering creative potential that individuals can use in their approach to dance and movement.

Given the revolutionary nature of its history, modern dance is in a strong position to be one of the best dance techniques for developing creativity in dancers. Dance has been described as an art form in which a dancer moves through space and time with dynamic and expressive movement qualities. Our body structure and movement potential, our senses and emotions, and our life experiences, attitudes, and intentions all contribute to the way we move both in our daily life and in our dance movements. There are various movement exercises that you can do to develop your awareness of your postural body shapes, the interrelationships and connections of the body parts, your relationship to space, and how your energy and intentions affect movement qualities and expression.

FINDING NEW WAYS TO MOVE

Where does movement originate? An important primary source is yourself. Movement experienced with no expectation of right or wrong results can be an effective method to begin the development of your own movement style and to begin to know how you want to express your inner feelings through movement. It is important that you develop awareness of yourself and commit to the discovery of the uniqueness of your own body structure in order to find how your body structure enables you to move most effectively. It is also important to nurture your movement preferences and expressivity. If you involve yourself in the spirit of improvisation, eventually you will find the way of moving that "feels right" for your body, based on all you have experienced in life. Sensitive self-exploration fosters your own creative understanding. In addition, establishing a strong partnership with your teacher as your guide and mentor in conjunction with your own self-knowledge will increase your potential for achieving your dance goals and dreams.

Body Awareness Exercises   Here are some preliminary exercises that can help you get into the movement process:

1. Lie on the floor in a relaxed position. Be sensitive to your body.

2. Be aware of your breathing, inhaling and exhaling, and notice what is happening in your body as a result of the breathing cycle. Be aware of how the body is internally and externally shaping itself as a result of how you are breathing. Try breathing through the vertical, width, and breadth of the body separately and then breathing through all three dimensions simultaneously so you feel the body expanding in the dimensions in a way similar to the inflation and deflation of a balloon.

3. Take some time to think about and sense the weight of your body supported by the floor.

4. Without moving, think about each part of your body. Imagine how each part can move through space and how each part is related to the whole body. For example, your upper leg bone is inserted into the hip socket at the pelvis and can move in all directions with or without rotation. The upper leg bone is attached to the lower leg bone, which primarily bends in only one direction and is in turn attached at the ankle joint, which leads down into the various movable bones of the foot. Think about how the pelvis/hip and heel connection facilitates movement.

5. Think about the length of the spine and how it connects the trunk to the head down through the upper back and lower back and into the pelvis. Think about how the lower and upper spine connection facilitates movement.

6. With the legs extended, flexing and extending in the ankle joints, set the body into a rocking motion—and be aware of the heel, pelvis, head connections. Check your body to see if you are holding tensions anywhere.

7. With knees up and bent, pulled toward the pelvis, rock the pelvis forward, backward, and sideward. The forward and backward motion is like the pathway created by a playground swing; the sideward motion is like the sideward rotation of a car's steering wheel. Do the sideward motion alternating with one hip up and one hip down, and be aware of how the body is affected by pelvic initiation.

8. Quietly lie on the floor and reflect on a significant past event; remember where you were and what you felt about the occasion. Let this reflective imagery lead your body to an awareness of how you felt then and feel now.

Improvisational Exercises Following are some improvisational exercises that may supplement the work given in the classroom. Try to do them when you are alone. Allow yourself plenty of time with each part of an exercise so that you don't feel rushed. Don't feel that you have to accomplish something, because there are no right or wrong results. When you are doing improvisation, you are trying to find out as much about your body as possible while moving through space and time with energy and expression.

The first two exercises may help you get in touch with your own body, body weight, and body rhythm.

1. Start lying on the floor. Take some time to sense your body. Are there any tensions anywhere? Stretch your body from head to foot, open the arms and legs wide to the side, and then relax. Repeat several times. Try to get a sense of what is happening in the body as you stretch and relax. Next, be aware of the shape of your body and how each part relates to the other parts of your body. Move to new lying positions and again note the changing body shape and the relationship of the body parts

Next, lying on your back, be aware of each part of your body in contact with the floor. Be aware of the weight of your body. Slowly lift and then lower various parts of your body, for example, an arm, a leg, and parts of the torso. Be aware of the weight of the body part and the kind of energy required to lift and lower it. Try the same kind of actions while lying on your back and your sides, and be aware of how the movement actions are changed.

Next, to sense your breath rhythms and how the body lengthens and widens in space, take a few moments to concentrate on how your body moves when you inhale and exhale. Without forcing, lengthen your body from the top of the head to the toes as you inhale, and shorten your body from the head to the toes as you exhale. Repeat this a number of times and then vary the idea by widening your body as you inhale and narrowing your body as you exhale. Finally, imagine the inner space of the torso as a large bell. Vocalize the vowels a, e, i, o, u and try to sense the sound as an internal changing body shape that is filling up the inner volume of the body. Explore the sound as originating from the areas of the pelvis, abdomen, chest, neck, or head. Be aware of how the sound, your breath, and your body all mutually support one another.

Next, to get a sense of your own rhythm, gently roll each part of your body from side to side on the floor—the head, a leg, an arm, the torso, and so forth. Be aware of the sensation of the movement and your body in contact with the floor. Next, gently roll the whole body from side to side and eventually roll over like a log being rolled. Next, to get a sense of your body weight working with gravity, again be aware of your breathing. As you inhale lift your head off the floor, and as you exhale lower the head to the floor. Without straining as you inhale, lift the pelvis off the floor, and as you exhale let the movement subside onto the floor. Repeat this action with the whole torso, being aware of the length of the spine. Continue this rising and lowering, rising higher with each inhalation until you come to a standing position.

2. Standing up, try to be free of any unnecessary tension in your body. Stand as still as possible and try to determine whether any subtle, involuntary motion is taking place in your body in response to the demands of standing upright. Try the same thing standing on both feet with eyes closed, standing on one foot, and standing on the balls of the feet. Next, again be aware of your breathing. Without forcing, lengthen your body upward as you inhale, and lower your body as you exhale. Next, as you inhale rise to the balls of your feet and stretch your arms overhead; as you exhale fall forward and catch your weight on one foot. Return to standing on both feet. Shift your pelvis forward in order to fall forward; again, shifting the pelvis in each direction, fall to each side and to the back. Repeat. Make certain the whole body is involved, and note the kind of energy you are using as you rise, fall, and recover. Repeat the action again with a rhythm of some kind—for example, rise, fall, recover, pause; rise, fall, recover, pause. Next, try varying the rhythm, for example, rise-rise-rise (slow), fall (fast), recover (fast) or rise (fast), fall-fall-fall (slow), recover (fast). The rate or speed of the movement may change its dynamics or quality. If so, try to sense how your body adapts to the changing dynamics.

3. This exercise may help you get a sense of the space around your body and how you can move through it. Stand quietly and visualize all the space around your body in front, in back, to the sides, above, and below. Imagine that the space has the consistency of the sculptor's modeling clay. From every direction, gather the space into yourself. Then mold or give shape to the imaginary clay—for example, various sizes of spheres, cubes, and so forth. Clearly indicate the size and weight of the molded object. Be aware of the rhythm of your actions as you knead, shape, pat, and smooth the "clay." Next, tear the molded space into small pellets and hurl them or scatter them individually in every direction around your body.

Next, try scattering or throwing imaginary objects, for example, a feather, a leaf, a marble, a shotput, a coin, or a piece of paper. Be aware of the kind of energy required in order to throw each object. Next, imagine how each object would move through space and settle to the ground. Imagining your body as the thrown object, try to move and settle the same way. Involve the whole body, and make the movements as broad as possible. This exercise should help you avoid making fragmented movements.

4. This exercise can help you develop a movement phrase. Select one word from each list in Table 6.1 and write the ten words sequentially on paper. Without preplanning, move your whole body in the way the ten-word description suggests. Keep repeating the sequence until you have a phrase that feels natural to you and that seems to have a beginning, a middle, and an end.

Write down two more word sequences with one word selected from each of the ten columns. Develop two more movement phrases. When you have established three movement phrases, try to give each one a beginning, a conclusion, and a transition into the next sequence. Decide whether any of the movements could be enriched by being performed another way and whether some movements ought to be eliminated or repeated a number of times. "Editing" one's work is an important function of the choreographer. Movements must be discarded if they do not contribute to the whole phrase or theme.

5. Initiate a series of movements by isolating one part of the body and using that part as an impetus to set your body in motion. The body part propels you through space in some direction, and you follow through until the movement comes to a conclusion. For example, let the head thrust backward, forward, or sideward, and let the rest of the body follow after the head has initiated the motion. Try the same with the pelvis, whole torso, shoulders, arms, legs, and so forth. Try moving in all of the different directions around your body.

6. Playing a game of red light/green light, move about the room quickly on the imaginary green light and come abruptly to a stop on the imaginary red light. Vary the timing of the stops and starts, and be aware of how your body reacts to the time element.

7. Imagine yourself walking in a swimming pool with the water up to your neck; then imagine yourself as an astronaut walking through weightless space. Be aware of how one restricts and the other frees the flow of your movement.

8. Imagine yourself in a vat of grapes. Crush the grapes with your feet; then lightly step on the grapes in another vat so that you do not crush any of them. Be aware of how your pelvis and center of gravity are involved in your exploration of weight.

9. Choose a spot in the room, and with total focus and attention go directly to that spot. Next, walk forward while reaching behind you with one arm and looking to the side at some spot in the room. Try to focus your attention on all three directions at the same time, setting up a spatial conflict between your desire and intention to go in all three directions at once. Ask yourself how this affects your attitude toward directness and indirectness in the space you are moving through.

TABLE 6.1   Constructing a Movement Phrase

Time	Body shape	Movement direction	Floor pattern	Mood feeling
slow	spread out	over	figure eight	alert
very slow	closed in	under	zigzag	vivacious
fast	large	through	branched out	calm
very fast	small	across	meander	joyful
slow-fast	tall	open out	circle	jovial
fast-slow	short	toward	spiral in	proud
sustained	curved	away	spiral out	bold
sudden	angular	rise	wavelike	courageous
leisurely	thin	sink	straight	flirtatious
rushed	stout	side	diagonal	triumphant
held back	growing	diagonal	square	vital
held	diminishing	around	triangle	

Image	Action	Action	Position in room	Mood feeling
melting	crouch	pull	center	agitated
floating	throw	press	front of center	sheepish
jerky	catch	strike	back of center	repulsed
bumpy	crawl	slash	left of center	nervous
bubbling	drop	dab	left front	defiant
pulsating	swing	flick	left back	furtive
sprinting	rock	pound	right of center	terrified
smooth	turn	shake	right front	giddy
light	bounce	squeeze	right back	pompous
heavy	jump	wring		surly
free	stretch	glide		brooding
restrained	twist	pounce		impatient

Exercises Combining Emotions, Ideas, Images, and Atmosphere   Emotions, ideas, images, and atmosphere can be used separately or together, or they can be combined with other approaches. Here are some examples of their use together:

1. Imagine yourself in a room full of strangers on a hot, humid day. Thread your way through the room without touching the people. Exaggerate the adjustments your body makes to avoid contact.

2. Imagine yourself in a brightly lit room. Suddenly the lights go out; you hear strange noises that you finally realize are being made by the walls closing in on you. The walls close in until they have forced you into a tiny ball on the floor. Express your reactions to these events with movements that are as exaggerated as you can make them.

3. Move your whole body broadly through some everyday actions, such as brushing your teeth, sewing, clipping your nails, brushing your hair, or twisting the cap off a bottle.

4. Crouch on the floor, making yourself as small as possible. Then slowly unfold your body and spread out in every direction until you fill the entire room. Now reverse the action. Repeat the sequence, with a sense of joy as you rise and a sense of grief as you descend. Repeat again, rising like a roaring brush fire and descending as if your body had turned to liquid.

5. Remember how you felt this morning when you got out of bed. Walking around the room, try to get the same feeling in your movements. Exaggerate the movements and sustain the mood as you walk freely around the room.

USING IMPROVISATION IN THE CLASSROOM

Solo, duet, and group improvisation might or might not be used by your teacher in some way in the classroom. Some teachers at some point in the training process introduce improvisation as another approach to developing your awareness of working with a partner or a group. In the mid-1970s, contact improvisation became a performance form in dance with similarities in movement to the improvisation of musicians with sound or actors with words.

Partner Awareness Exercises   Following are exercises that can be tried out with a dance classmate. Take your time doing the exercises. Be aware of and sensitive to your partner's movements and to how, cooperatively, you can make the movement experience meaningful to each of you. Face your partner in each exercise.

Weight

1. Face each other about three feet apart, feet comfortably balanced, arms forward and slightly bent with palms resting against your partner's palms. Take turns passively leaning forward into your partner's palms, allowing your partner to support your weight. Try to develop a trust in passively giving your body weight and receiving your partner's body weight.

2. Balance yourself with your one leg forward and one leg backward. As above, with palms together take turns actively pressing your weight against your partner's palms. Try to develop a sense of the give and

take of sharing the pressure of actively using your own body weight or actively yielding to the body weight of your partner.

3. With feet comfortably together and knees bent, hold hands at the wrist and lean back away from each other. Experiment with sensitively using each other's weight to oppositionally shift the weight forward, backward, and sideward, eventually cooperatively moving downward, with control, to sit on the floor.

Leading and Following

1. Facing each other with only the fingertips touching, take turns slowly moving, with one partner doing a free pattern of movement and the other following. Explore the space in front of you upward, downward, and sideward. Explore different spatial patterns, both linear and circular.

2. Facing each other a comfortable distance apart, repeat exercise 1 above without being in contact. Think of your movements as being a mirror image of your partner's movements. As you move, be sensitive to allowing your partner to sense, anticipate, and follow your moves. Take your time and allow your partner to share in your movement qualities and choices.

Tips for Classroom Improvisation

If your teacher works with improvisation, he or she will have a particular way of conducting improvisations. Some teachers incorporate them into a technique class, while others include them in a separate composition class or some other format. In beginning improvisation, some dancers feel shy or embarrassed about moving freely in front of others in the class. This feeling can be overcome. The sooner it is overcome, the more pleasure and rewards will result from the experience.

When your teacher gives you directions for an improvisation, listen carefully. When you are ready to begin, do not plan your movements ahead of time. Let them flow naturally based on the instructions given. Try to stay within the structure outlined. Avoid trying to imitate some movement sequence you have seen or learned elsewhere. Try to let things happen naturally without forcing them to happen. Don't be concerned about how the movement looks to others who might be watching. Concentrate on what you are doing. Remember that this is your own movement experience and that later your teacher can give you helpful suggestions. The more you improvise, the easier it becomes.

Whether or not your teacher does improvisation does not matter;

exploring some of the ideas suggested in this chapter can help you find a way of moving that is unique because it originates from you and you alone.

BENEFITS OF IMPROVISATION

Improvisation can be focused in many different ways to achieve different goals and to develop your dance appreciation and awareness. Some of the benefits of improvisation are:

1. Immediate accumulation, analysis, and synthesis of information to make decisions about movement, space, time, groupings, and group interactions.
2. Discovery of new movement and a lessening of reliance on preconceived ideas about movement.
3. Development of your awareness as a performer.
4. Experience of various concepts of movement and dance.
5. Development of your creative responses within the performance structure.
6. Development and use of a movement vocabulary.
7. Refinement of sensory and rhythmical acuity.
8. Development of movement recall for choreography.
9. Exploration of the senses, emotions, and feeling states.
10. Increased knowledge and understanding of the body in space and time.
11. Development of receptiveness to others when working within a group.
12. Development of the ability to find creative solutions to challenges.
13. Introduction to the choreographic process and structure.

Not only will improvisation enrich your dance experience, but it will also carry over into other areas of your life and help you develop an ability to use creativity in problem solving.

Chapter 7
Choreographic Approaches

Each dance is unique and free, a separate organism
whose form is self-determined.

MARY WIGMAN

Mark Morris Dance Group, "Dido and Aeneas." Photo by D. Pierre.

Some students ask, "Why should I study choreography when all I want to do is dance?" It's true that a brilliant dancer may never have choreographed anything, and a brilliant choreographer may have been a poor dancer. A successful performer, however, doesn't just dance. You dance about something or to express something, even when the dance is without a plot. If you hope to make a statement with your body that reflects your intentions or those of the choreographer, you should have some idea of the choreographic structure behind the dance you are doing. If you want to teach dancing or to choreograph someday, you can save yourself countless hours of aimless experimentation by knowing a few techniques for how to begin your experiments.

Improvisation and basic choreographic forms might be as much a part of your training as daily technique classes. Technique classes train the body. Improvisation frees your movement from the restrictions placed on it by a codified technique and frees your own creative energies. Knowledge of choreographic structures trains your mind and sharpens your critical faculties and perceptions.

There are many ways to choreograph. You will find the way that works best for you. We present here only a few basic approaches to choreographic exploration.

DESIGN

A sense of body design in space and good stage balance comes with experience. You can do a number of things to develop your "artistic eye" for line, form, shape, and theatrical drama.

Observing Design   Pictures are telegraphic. They tell you a story without the addition of a caption below them. Dance should be able to do the same. Try the following exercises to help develop your artistic eye:

1. Look at paintings of different periods of history. Observe how the artist has placed the people in relationship to one another, how the people are posed, and why their clothes make them stand out the way they do.

2. Study the pictures in a pictorial magazine such as *Life* and see why some pictures and advertisements hold your attention.

3. Look at the pictures of athletes in "frozen" motion and trace the natural lines of their movement.

4. Look at the buildings or the landscape around you and ask what is beautiful, interesting, or jarring about it.

If you want to dance about people and their universal concerns, you have to understand them and what makes them behave as they do in a given set of circumstances. The following exercises are a study of people and nature:

1. Watch how people of different ages and social classes walk, sit, and stand.

2. Observe how people move when they are happy, sad, or expressing some other emotion.

3. Watch how people in a social situation group themselves into a circle or how some sit off by themselves.

4. Watch how children, animals, and birds move and consider why they move that way.

5. Study the shapes formed by a tree, a leaf, a rock, or oil stains on a mud puddle.

6. Become acutely aware of your own senses. How do different textures feel? Be aware of odors, notice the taste of your food, really study how something looks (its shapes, its colors), and start to listen carefully to the sounds of nature and to man-made sounds.

7. Begin to notice natural movements, such as the sway of trees, the ebb and flow of waves, and the ripples in a pond. Try to sense the dynamics of the motion and how your body could suggest that movement and its dynamics.

All of life, all of nature, is potentially the concern of the artist, who must bring some kind of order out of the myriad possibilities through selection and emphasis. Basically, choreography can be thought of as planning movement of the human body through space and time. It requires choices in body movement and spatial design, rate of speed, rhythm, dynamics, and overall form. To have merit, the materials of dance need to be manipulated imaginatively rather than as a series of movements strung together without coherence. Developing appropriate movements takes time and discipline.

Choreographers work in many different ways, some letting the dance shape itself, others having clearly established ideas they wish to communicate. For the beginning choreographer, it is usually helpful to define the theme of your study or work. It is helpful to consider what the content of the study will be, how it will develop logically, and what it will communicate. All sections should flow naturally into one another and should have coherence to the whole.

Kinds of Design   There are two basic modes of stage design: symmetrical and asymmetrical. In symmetrical design, the stage is equally balanced on both sides. For example, if you have two dancers on one side of the stage, then you have two dancers on the other side. In asymmetrical design, the stage is not balanced. If you have two dancers on one side of the stage, you might have four on the other side in staggered positions. Symmetrical design is the most pleasing to look at, but it becomes the dullest to look at if overused. Another kind of design is dynamic design achieved by linear spacing of dancers or massed grouping; the first establishes the line, the second a sense of volume or mass.

Dynamic design

Presumably you are choreographing for members of an audience, so you want to keep their eyes constantly "entertained" with unexpected movements, lines, shapes, and forms. There is nothing worse than putting your audience to sleep. There are no bad audiences—only bad dancers and bad choreographers. You have a responsibility to communicate something to a paying audience even if it is outraged at what you have done. The worst thing you can do to your audience is cause indifference or boredom, unless that is your intention.

MOTIVE AND CHARACTER

Another approach to finding new movement or to defining a character in a dance work is to improvise by working from human stereotypes, from the psychological makeup of a specific person, or from gestures or common movement activities such as throwing a ball or by using an animal as a reference point for character definition.

If you are going to choreograph a part—a swaggering braggart, for example—you could ask yourself questions such as what motivates this person, what does he want, and how does he move. An easy way to begin is to decide that he acts like some animal, maybe a strutting rooster. You could then improvise around the idea of a rooster strutting with his chest pushed forward and his head quickly surveying all of his domain.

Gesture   A different approach to defining a braggart's character with movement is to improvise on some imaginary situation he might be in.

For example, if he were in a room full of people and was offered food, how would he take the food from a tray and how would he eat it?

If the movement is to be repeated and set into a dance for the character, it is helpful to decide first on a few extreme examples of how this person moves, or exaggerated postures that he might assume, and then combine them, moving from one extreme posture to another or from movement pattern to movement pattern. You can eventually arrive at specific movements that get your idea across. The tendency with novice choreographers is to put everything they know indiscriminately into the dance. An audience will probably see the choreography only once and so must be carefully led to see the idea that you want them to see.

Abstraction of Character   You will not always choreograph or dance as a literal, recognizable character; sometimes you will dance or choreograph as an abstraction of an idea or character. The same methods of choreographic improvisation and definition described above can be utilized until you have arrived at the essence of what you want to say in movement. For example, if you pick a flower from a garden, you could go through the actual motions of picking a flower (literal gesture) or a stylized motion of picking a flower (pantomime) or an extended motion suggesting the picking of a flower, indicating the joy or nostalgia you feel rather than the actual picking of the flower (dance).

Emotion or Feeling   Sometimes it is useful to develop a movement motif that originates from your feelings. An example of a process working with feeling is to find and listen to a recording of a piece of music that evokes strong feelings or elicits some kind of imagery for you. Get in a comfortable position and listen to your selected music. Using crayons or colored felt pens, without preplanning, freely make patterns on a large blank piece of paper that are expressive of your feelings and your response to the music. Next, using some flexible colored wire, create a three-dimensional sculpture of the pattern you drew on the paper. When you have created the sculpture, move through the pattern from one end to the other. Do this until you have a repeatable movement pattern. As you are doing the movement pattern, try to bring your initial feelings into the movement.

Object   Sometimes it is useful to use an object that you find has a beautiful pattern—for example, a seashell, a dried branch from a tree, a crystal, or a sculpture. Trace your finger over the pattern many times until you have discovered the details of the pattern. See if you can find what the object symbolizes as a theme for you. By moving through the pattern while expressing your symbolic theme, you can establish a movement motif that has meaning for you.

Action Picture From newspapers or magazines, find four or five still photographs of dancers or athletes caught in the frozen moment of an exciting action sequence. Attach the still photos to a blank paper in a sequence that you find interesting. Organically move from one static pose to the next, developing a spatial movement pattern that has a natural ebb and flow. Experiment with the change between poses in order to develop an exciting movement pattern. In performing your pattern, try to capture the spirit of what you originally found appealing in the spatial tensions and designs suggested in the photos.

FORMS

Many people have ideas but lack the ability to share them with others. You as a choreographer or dancer must develop the craft of organizing your ideas into some structure that will communicate them to the audience.

There is no easy formula that will guarantee success, but a few forms around which you can organize your ideas are presented here as possible starting points. (Some of these basic forms require more than one dancer.)

Theme The theme is one of the most elemental forms. It is particularly useful when you begin to choreograph extended pieces. A theme makes some basic statement and is organized around some central movement idea. For example, using the idea of a "work theme," you could choreograph a movement pattern of eight bars suggesting the movements of a lumberman chopping down a tree. The movement theme: He chops the tree.

Theme and Variation The basic movement theme is shown once and then repeated with some kind of basic change. Common ways of doing the variation are:

1. Slowing down the entire movement pattern.
2. Speeding up the entire movement pattern.
3. Inverting the movement (for example, movements that go up now go down, movements that came toward the body now go away from the body).
4. Reversing the movement pattern (that is, starting at the end and working toward the beginning).
5. Extending the amount of time selected movements are performed.
6. Diminishing the amount of time selected movements are performed.

7. Embellishing or adding movement to the basic theme.

8. Eliminating movement from the basic theme.

Starting with the basic chopping theme and then doing each of these eight variations for eight bars, you would end up with a choreographic piece seventy-two bars long. In embellishing the basic theme, you might add the idea that the lumberman stops to wipe his brow with a handkerchief because of the heat or stops to sharpen the cutting blade or to watch the tree fall. By combining the basic theme with variations or with some other form, you can tell a story or suggest a change of mood or anything that you want to communicate, yet beneath it all is a basic structure that has a unity with your basic premise, the original eight bars of movement.

ABA   Another common form is ABA—the statement of a basic theme (A), a second theme (B), and a repetition of the original theme (A). The lumberman is chopping briskly with a steady rhythm in the first theme; in the second theme he tires, and the chopping slows down and changes rhythm frequently; then he gets a "second wind" and again chops briskly with a steady rhythm.

Fugue   The fugue requires more than one dancer. For example, you start with a basic theme of chopping for eight bars. These original eight bars are repeated exactly the same way by the same dancer or other dancers throughout the entire piece, while the original dancer or some other dancer or dancers do variations on the original theme.

Sonata   The sonata form is made up of two themes, primary and secondary, plus a recapitulation or joining of the two themes. For example, in theme 1 the man chops the tree. In theme 2 the man watches the tree fall. In the recapitulation, the man again chops the tree and watches it fall. In such a recapitulation of the two themes, you might have the idea of felling a forest and not merely one tree.

Round   The round is a common form exemplified by the song "Three Blind Mice." The same theme is repeated a number of times, with new dancers joining in at some point. The beginning dancer finishes first, then the other dancers stop as they finish the same movement pattern. For example, the man chops the tree (movement A), the man wipes his brow (movement B), and the man watches the tree fall (movement C). In a simple round, the first dancer starts at movement A, continues through movements B and C, and stops. The second dancer begins at movement A when the first dancer begins movement B and continues to the end and stops. The third dancer begins movement A when the second dancer begins at movement B and continues to the end and stops. The first dancer, instead of stopping at the end of movement C, may introduce new movement themes that are repeated by the second and third dancers.

Canon   The canon form is similar to the round except that all the dancers finally join in the same movement to bring it to an end (coda). In a dance canon, each new dancer does the movement exactly as the original movement was done, but the new dancer may be a different physical or emotional type from the original dancer. In the original theme, the lumberman chops the tree. In the successive repeats of the theme, he may be joined by his wife and then by his son.

Counterpoint   In counterpoint, two independent themes are danced against one another. The lumberman chops the tree while someone builds a house using the material the lumberman has produced.

Chance Composition   Choreography by chance is called a form here because the artist must still select and shape the final piece. One common example is placing a certain number of movement instructions written on individual pieces of paper into a box, then drawing them out one at a time and assembling them into a movement pattern in the same order they were drawn out. For example, you might draw out these instructions: (1) Move in a circle, (2) make percussive movements, and (3) exhale. Using the idea of the lumberman, you might have him circle the tree, chop it sharply, and exhale with fatigue. It should be understood, however, that choreography by chance usually implies the lack of a preconceived theme.

   All of these forms could, of course, be built around some other theme—abstract, literal, or movement oriented.

TIME AND MUSIC

Time   As a choreographer, you need to develop an awareness of your personal sense of time, that is, your own inner rhythm that motivates the time duration of your movements. Your creative organization of the timing of the movements can enrich your choreographic expression. In one sense, time can be thought of metaphorically as a stream of water connecting what has been, what is now, and what will be in the future. Time has been associated with the changing seasons and years and more recently with the ever-present clock. Time is an important element of dance. How you perceive and structure the time elements in your choreography will influence how you interpret your personal perspective and convey it to both your dancers and the audience.

Music Traditionally, dance is performed to music or to structured sound of some kind. You may use prerecorded music, work with musicians or a composer, or create your own music or organized sounds. Whatever method you choose to use, it is important to know some of the language of music and how it is organized. Musicians do not necessarily know the language of dance, but dancers need to know about music. Your knowledgeable and creative interpretation of music or organized sound will enhance your choreographic intentions. One way of learning more about this craft is to follow a musical score while listening to the prerecorded score.

Measure Music is organized into bars (measures). In the examples that follow, we have listed the most common musical meters that you are likely to encounter in your beginning work. (Notice that the "and" counts have been omitted.) The symbol > indicates the strong beat. The symbol ⌐ indicates the secondary or moderate beat, which means that it is accented more heavily than the other counts but not as heavily as the strong beat. The two numbers written as a fraction constitute the musical time signature. The upper number shows how many counts there are in a bar, and the lower number shows what kind of durational value gets one count. In 2/4 time, for example, there are two counts to a bar and a quarter note gets one count. In dance, the upper number is more important.

Rhythm Try clapping the following rhythms, accenting the first count to get their rhythmical feeling.

$$\frac{4}{4} \quad \overset{>}{1} \quad 2 \quad \overset{˘}{3} \quad 4 \; | \; \overset{>}{1} \quad 2 \quad \overset{˘}{3} \quad 4 \; | \; \overset{>}{1} \quad 2 \quad \overset{˘}{3} \quad 4$$

(three bars of four counts each)

$$\frac{3}{4} \quad \overset{>}{1} \quad 2 \quad 3 \; | \; \overset{>}{1} \quad 2 \quad 3 \; | \; \overset{>}{1} \quad 2 \quad 3$$

$$\frac{2}{4} \quad \overset{>}{1} \quad 2 \; | \; \overset{>}{1} \quad 2 \; | \; \overset{>}{1} \quad 2$$

$$\frac{6}{8} \quad \overset{>}{1} \quad 2 \quad 3 \quad \overset{˘}{4} \quad 5 \quad 6 \; | \; \overset{>}{1} \quad 2 \quad 3 \quad \overset{˘}{4} \quad 5 \quad 6 \; | \; \overset{>}{1} \quad 2 \quad 3 \quad \overset{˘}{4} \quad 5 \quad 6$$

Notice that the 6/8 rhythm has been stressed heavily on the first count and less heavily on the fourth count. Often a 6/8 rhythm is played very quickly by the musician, so it is frequently more easily counted by the teacher as $\overset{>}{1}$ 2 | $\overset{>}{1}$ 2 or $\overset{>}{1}$ and a $\overset{>}{2}$ and a.

The example below shows how the counts would be written in musical notation.

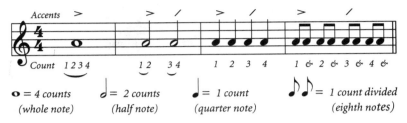

$\mathbf{o}$ = 4 counts
(whole note)

$\mathbf{d}$ = 2 counts
(half note)

$\mathbf{\downarrow}$ = 1 count
(quarter note)

= 1 count divided
(eighth notes)

The modern dancer often experiments with changes in the rhythmical form. You may change the number of counts in the basic musical bars to give variety. You might dance to a series of bars such as 1̇ 2   3 | 1̇ 2   3   4 | or 1̇ 2 | 1̇ 2   3 or some other combination of rhythms. This is referred to as *mixed meter*.

Another musical change you might use is called *shifted accent*. Instead of falling on the first count, the accent falls on another count. For example:

1̇   2   3 | 1   2̇   3 | 1   2̇   3 | 1   2   3̇

1   2   3̇ | 1̇   2̇   3 | 1̇   2   3 | 1̇   2   3

Here the expected heavy accent in the third, fourth, fifth, and sixth bars has been shifted to a count other than the first count. This example shows a rhythmic concept called *syncopation*—a displacement of accents onto beats of the measure that are not usually emphasized.

Cumulative rhythm occurs when each succeeding bar has one more count added to it. For example: 1̇ | 1̇ 2 | 1̇ 2 3 | 1̇ 2 3 4. *Subtractive rhythm* is the exact opposite of cumulative rhythm. Each succeeding bar has one count subtracted from it. For example: 1̇ 2 3 4 | 1̇ 2 3 | 1̇ 2 | 1̇.

Hemiola is a regular displacement of accent that temporarily produces a new time signature. For example: ⁶⁄₈ 1̇ 2 3̇ 4 5̇ 6.

Dancers do not always dance with the strong recurring beat of the music. This would soon lead to boredom. To add interest, the dancers also move on the "offbeat" or against the prevailing rhythm. If you clap the counts below with the accents indicated above them, you will feel the sense of *double time,* or doubling of the basic beat. Each bar should take exactly the same amount of time to clap:

1̇ 2 3̇ 4, 1̇ and 2 and 3̇ and 4 and, 1̇ 2 3̇ 4, 1̇ and 2 and 3̇ and 4 and

Common groupings of counts (musical notes) in a measure used in dancing are groups of 2s (2/4 time, two quarter notes, with two strong beats, or 6/8 time, six eighth notes, with two strong beats, each with sub-beats of 3), 3s (3/4 time), or 4s (4/4 time). See the examples below (a small u indicates an unaccented beat):

$$\frac{2}{4} \quad \overset{>}{1} \quad \overset{u}{2} \mid \overset{>}{1} \quad \overset{u}{2}$$

$$\frac{3}{4} \quad \overset{>}{1} \quad \overset{u}{2} \quad \overset{u}{3} \mid \overset{>}{1} \quad \overset{u}{2} \quad \overset{u}{3}$$

$$\frac{4}{4} \quad \overset{>}{1} \quad \overset{u}{2} \quad \overset{>}{3} \quad \overset{u}{4} \mid \overset{>}{1} \quad \overset{u}{2} \quad \overset{>}{3} \quad \overset{u}{4}$$

$$\frac{6}{8} \quad \overset{>}{1} \text{ and } \overset{u}{a} \quad \overset{>}{2} \text{ and } \overset{u}{a} \mid \overset{>}{1} \text{ and } \overset{u}{a} \quad \overset{>}{2} \text{ and } \overset{u}{a}$$

Another common musical grouping used in modern dance is the *triplet*—three quick movements done to one count of music:

$$\frac{3}{4} \quad \begin{array}{l} \text{dance count:} \\ \text{music count:} \end{array} \quad \underbrace{1 \quad 2 \quad 3}_{1} \mid \underbrace{1 \quad 2 \quad 3}_{2} \mid \underbrace{1 \quad 2 \quad 3}_{3}$$

Dancers sometimes prefer to group a series of musical measures together to go with a longer phrase of dance movement, for example, an eight-count phrase combining two measures of 4/4 time. Or, in a fast 3/4 time such as a waltz, dancers may count each measure of three counts as only one count:

$$\frac{3}{4} \quad \begin{array}{l} \text{dance count:} \\ \text{music count:} \end{array} \quad \overbrace{\underset{1 \quad 2 \quad 3}{1}} \mid \overbrace{\underset{1 \quad 2 \quad 3}{2}} \mid \overbrace{\underset{1 \quad 2 \quad 3}{3}} \mid$$

To get a feeling in your body of these musical concepts, connect the mixed-meter, shifted-accent, syncopation, and cumulative and subtractive rhythms into a movement phrase. Use broad, strong movements to illustrate each strong accent so that the structure of each bar is clear.

Tempo Tempo refers to the speed of the musical accompaniment or dance movement. *Changes in tempo* from very slow to very fast or the reverse result in a change of the quality of the movement. Changes in tempo sometimes make otherwise dreary movement quite exciting to watch.

Common musical tempi, from very slow to very fast, are largo, lento, adagio, andante, moderato, allegro, vivace, presto. To keep track of where you are in the music and movement phrase, it might be helpful to number the measures as you are working, for example, measures 1234, 2234, 3234, 4234, and so forth.

MUSIC AND DANCE COMPOSITION

Music can add a great deal to your choreography, or it can destroy it. Following are a few things to keep in mind when you are working with music. (You might want to choreograph the dance in *opposition* to these ideas in order to achieve a dissonant look in your movement.)

1. Keep the qualities of the dance movement consistent with the mood of the music (or, for contrast, deliberately work against the mood of the music).

2. Analyze the structure of the music so that you can repeat the movements on the same counts or phrases twice running or so that you can teach the movement to someone else without being vague about what happens when. A pencil and paper are invaluable. Make dashes on the paper in accompaniment with the regular beats of the music until you have developed some kind of musical pattern to work from. As you listen over and over to the music, make notes above the dashes to indicate shifts in the rhythm, shifts in the mood, or the appearance of new instruments—or whatever other notes can guide you.

3. Try composing your own music. You might play it *while you are dancing* or have someone play it for you. You can use percussion instruments if they are available. If not, so much the better: Find and use rocks, sticks, or dried leaves on a branch, or run a comb over paper. You can discover exciting new sounds by trying out the least likely objects. Then organize the sounds into some repeatable form. If you have access to a tape recorder, you can record your music. A tape recorder makes it possible to use other sounds as well, for example, a ticking clock, an airplane, dripping water, or a cat's cry. Composing your own music frees you from the restrictions placed on you by the composer, and it can also be a lot of fun.

4. Find your own way of working with music that is best suited to your own creative needs. Ideally, dancers and choreographers need to know as much as possible about the wide range of types of music, both historical and contemporary, available to them and about what kind of instruments produce what kind of sounds. Radio, television, and recorded music are good sources for hearing music, from symphonic compositions to the latest musical innovations. Television is a good source for hearing and seeing which instrument is producing which sounds.

Anyone interested in choreographing should keep a journal to notate information about music that might be good for choreographing. In the same journal, you could jot down ideas or sketches of movement images you have. These jottings could be a useful resource at a later time.

COSTUMES, PROPS, AND SCENERY

If you are going to wear a costume or use scenery and props, take advantage of them by analyzing their function in relation to your purposes. For example, if you are wearing a long cape, experiment to find out how many different ways you can move it or use it to augment the spatial designs of your body. Can it be used as a prop like a bullfighter's cape or placed on the floor to suggest a forbidden territory that no one dares to enter? The important thing to remember about a dance costume is that you don't just wear it but rather take advantage of its restrictions and use them to enhance your visual designs or enhance your ideas.

Costumes do not need to be expensive in order to be effective. Using your leotard and tights as a basic costume, you can perform wonders with pieces of unsewn material or dyes.

If you use stage props, explore all their possibilities. For example, an ordinary chair can be sat on, lain on, stood on, crawled under or over, or danced with like a silent partner. The list of uses is endless.

Costumes, props, and scenery make it possible to extend the potentials of your body design in space and to add new elements of stage interest. The only limitations to movement possibilities are those that come either from your not being imaginative or from your deliberately being selective.

If you become discouraged in your experiments, keep in mind that even the most famous choreographers started at the beginning. No less than they, you have to work at your craft if you want eventually to use it to express your ideas and feelings.

FOCUS

As a choreographer, you need to establish for yourself and your audience the primary objective of the piece and how all the parts relate to the *basic focus* or purpose. In developing your dance movement, you and your dancers will need to find an *internal focus* and intention that motivates it. It is also important to clearly define for the dancers the *external focus* to the space and to the other dancers. As a choreographer, you need to develop your awareness of the spatial arrangement and the spatial movement of the dancers on the stage. They must know where, when, how, and why they enter or exit the performance space. Finally, you need to direct the *audience's focus* to what you want them to see at any given time.

Whether or not you intend to become a professional choreographer, you can gain knowledge about yourself and about the art of dance by developing organized movements into a piece that has meaning for you. Merce Cunningham once said to just keep choreographing, and one day you will wake up to find that you have become a choreographer. Doris Humphrey stood quietly in the studio freeing herself of all she had learned and waited for the person in the mirror to reveal her own personal potential movement. Paul Taylor, as a student of art, brought his knowledge of art to his choreography. Alwin Nikolais brought his knowledge of music and technology to the development of a new way of organizing movement into a dance art. Choreographing is not like using a cookbook, turning to a page to find your recipe; it is a whole way of life.

You can learn the craft of choreography, but only you can bring your unique point of view to the creation of a dance work that is based on all you have experienced in your lifetime.

Chapter 8
Evaluation and Criticism

We have to meet the artist halfway. We have to bring
something before we can bring something away.

CLIVE BARNES

Donald McKayle Dance Company

Often you hear people say of something they have seen, "I liked it" or "I didn't like it." This is the beginning of criticism. Unfortunately, most people never go beyond these statements to analyze *why* they liked or didn't like what they saw.

If you want to dance, choreograph, teach, or simply be an intelligent member of the audience, it is important to know why you liked or didn't like something and to be able to express your viewpoint intelligently. You can learn a great deal about what to do and what not to do in the dance theater by seeing dance concerts and by critically evaluating what you have seen. Your criticisms should never be exclusively negative or positive. You should impartially evaluate both the good and the bad features.

You may not be able to see dance concerts regularly, but you can increase your critical faculties and perceptions in other ways. Every movie, television show, advertisement, short story, and so on has a structure and makes a statement in some way, good or bad. You can apply the same principles to these communication forms that you do to dance. Each time you see a dance work, you are increasing your ability to judge and critique a dance.

CRITERIA FOR EVALUATION

You can analyze the overall structure by asking yourself how it began, how it ended, and what happened in between. A well-structured dance should have a beginning, a development of the beginning, and a resolution. The form may or may not be used to tell a story. Nevertheless, it should start somewhere, accomplish something, and be resolved.

With a professional company, you have the right to ask if the work was performed well and if the dancers contributed to the choreographer's conception. Many good works are ruined by bad dancers, and many bad works are effective when performed by good dancers. Was it theatrically exciting? There is no law that says art cannot be entertaining. The audience has a right to expect something more for its time and money than a pedestrian presentation of an idea.

Creative choreographers make a personal, unique dance statement that sets their dance work apart from other choreographers' works. In viewing a dance, you might be able to categorize it in a general way that will help you gain insights into the choreographer's perceptions about movement and how he or she has unified them into a cohesive whole. Does the work have a narrative story line, or is it abstract, with little or no attempt at pictorial representation? Do spectacle and technical display seem more important than the inventiveness of the dance movements? How have the choreographer and scenic and lighting designers established a mood, a locale, and an environment for bringing the viewer into the choreographer's vision? Has the choreographer used the music, sound, words, or silence in a way that reinforces both the audio and the visual aspects of the work?

Modern dance may be performed in many different kinds of performance spaces. The kinds of spaces used will influence the final shape of the dance. In developing your awareness and critical skills, it is helpful to analyze the performance space, how the choreographer has utilized the restrictions and potentials of that space, and whether or not the space has been transformed into an arena for theater-dance "magic" or something else.

Choreographers usually have a characteristic style achieved by the kind of movement choices they have made. Is the movement generally free, lyrical, and harmonious, is it restricted, angular, and disharmonious, or is it something else? How do the dancers move through the space, enter and exit, and organize themselves to the space or to the other dancers? How has the choreographer organized the duration of time and rhythm in the piece? What kind of emotions, moods, thoughts, or ideas do the dancers seem to be expressing, and are they expressing them through gestures, postures, or relationships among dancers, or in some other manner? How has the choreographer organized each section of the work, and how does each section relate to the whole?

The questions in the following lists can help you increase your critical and evaluative skills and give you ideas to consider when doing your own choreography.

The Dance as a Whole

1. Was there a unifying theme in the dance that could be identified? If so, what was it? If not, how could the choreographer have made it clearer?

2. Did the theme of the work have relevance for you? Why do you think the theme was important to the choreographer? Did the theme express something to which many people can relate? Why or why not?

3. What ideas were expressed in the dance for you? Did the title of the piece or the program notes appropriately reflect the ideas? How did your ideas of the dance and the title of the work agree or disagree?

4. Was there a sense of a beginning thematic idea being established, a development of this theme, and an end or resolution that brought the piece to a satisfactory conclusion that expressed the choreographer's point of view? If not, what was unclear in the beginning, middle, or

end of the work, and what might have clarified the choreographer's intention?

5. How did the choreographer use time, space, dynamics, silence-sound-music, theatrical "texture," the dancers' potential, and the performance space to establish a choreographic style?

6. Was there a characteristic style in the movement? Was the style consistent and coherent with the theme and ideas of the work? How would you characterize the style of the movement and how it related to the theme?

7. Was the choreographer appropriately creative in the use of movement and visual images and in establishing a compelling theatrical environment? Were there moments of surprise, tension, or humor, striking memorable visual images or sounds, or moments that strongly resonated with your own feelings? What moments in the piece stood out for you? Why?

8. Did the work succeed for you or the audience? Why?

9. Did the choreographer introduce a concept of performance that was different from what you had previously experienced? If so, in what way?

10. Did the work challenge you to think in terms of new concepts in the use of basic dance elements of space, time, and dynamics?

11. As the diverse world dances become more visible in our society, they sometimes have an influence on the work of some choreographers. Did the style of this work suggest any cross-cultural influences? If you are familiar with dances from other cultures, do they have an influence on your work? If so, how?

12. What are the ongoing challenges for artists working in the dance medium? How do your own goals relate to the works you are seeing and evaluating?

Technical Considerations

1. Did the technical support generally enhance the performance?

2. Did the music, sound, words, or silence enhance the theme? Was the sound too large or too small for the work? Was the music chopped and rearranged in a way that distorted the composer's purpose?

3. Were the lighting design and execution suitable for the piece? Was it too dark to see the dancers? Did the lights overpower the movement?

4. Did the costumes contribute to or detract from the piece? Could a

change of costume give an added dimension? Were the costumes manipulated well? Did they flatter the dancers' bodies?

5. Were the props an integral part of the work? Were they used in an imaginative manner? Did the dancers seem at ease with them?

6. Were the makeup and hair designs appropriate for the dance?

Performance Considerations

1. Were the dancers well trained for what they were asked to perform?

2. Did the dancers work well together during the performance?

3. Was the number of dancers appropriate for the piece?

4. Were the dancers involved with projecting the idea of the work rather than with their technique or their bodies?

5. Did the dancers seem to be well rehearsed?

6. Did the dancers seem secure and at ease with the movement and the piece?

Space Considerations

1. What is the space like? Is it a regular proscenium arch theater, a thrust stage, theater-in-the-round, a room, a studio, an outdoor platform, an outdoor environmental location, a building site, a television studio, or something else?

2. How has the performance been transformed by theatrical elements such as lighting or, in the case of an environmental setting, by natural or man-made elements present in the site?

3. How has the choreographer adapted the dance to the performance area to take advantage of a stage that is too large or not large enough, or to an environmental venue such as the seashore?

4. Because of the location, what is the relationship between the audience and the performers? How does that affect your perception of the dance? If you are seated in a theater, you will view the dance from only one viewpoint, whereas in the outdoors you might move around and see the dance from a number of viewpoints and angles.

5. If the dance has been created or restaged for television, what movements and how much of the dancer's body have been selected by the choreographer to be shown to the audience?

6. How do the potentials of the television medium differ from those of a live performance? How has the choreographer manipulated the movement images by using camera and recording techniques?

DEVELOPING YOUR CRITICAL FACULTIES

You may or may not like a performance, but you should be able to understand the choreographer's ideas and to appreciate the way the ideas were created and developed. If you didn't like it, ask yourself first if you came with a preconception of what dance is supposed to be and this company didn't live up to your expectations. If you want to develop your critical abilities and sensibilities, you have to be open to new ideas and new approaches in dance. Remember that many of the dance movements of the modern-dance pioneers were thought strange and ugly by an audience unaccustomed to this new way of moving.

Many times, the old rules do not readily apply to a work you have seen. Remember, the established methods and rules of choreography and performance are merely a foundation to be built upon. New ideas are constantly being created and developed. Some dances are composed to be antitheatrical, and some are performed in spaces other than a traditional theater or proscenium stage. For these reasons alone, the shape and content of modern dance keep changing. You don't have to accept as "great" everything you see, but you should know why you consider something great, mediocre, or merely pleasing.

Like the muscles of your body, your critical faculties and perceptions are developed by being used regularly. Just as incorrect training makes muscles undesirably bulky, a closed mind impedes both your creativity and stops the flow of new ideas in your evaluations and in your own work.

Keep in mind that as a member of the audience you are a vital part of the process of the art. The choreographer, the performers, and you collaborate in the completion of the work. The choreographer offers a vision that is created through the dancers and is given new meaning by your method of interpreting it and relating to it in terms of your own experiences. Your sincere attempt to really see what is happening, to understand the artist's vision, and to critically analyze the work from your own experiences will strengthen your evaluative abilities. The more dance you see and the more you practice analyzing what you see, the greater appreciation you will have for the dance, both as a critic and as a participant.

Selected References

PREPARATION

Ambrosio, Nora. (1994). *Learning about Dance: An Introduction to Dance as an Art Form and Entertainment.* Dubuque, Iowa: Kendall/Hunt Publishing Company.

Cheney, Gay. (1989). *Basic Concepts in Modern Dance: A Creative Approach.* Princeton, N.J.: Princeton Book Company.

DeMille, Agnes. (1962). *To a Young Dancer.* Boston and Toronto: Little, Brown.

Minton, Sandra Cerny. (1989). *Body and Self, Partners in Movement.* Champaign, Ill.: Human Kinetics Books.

ANATOMY

Berardi, Gigi. (1991). *Finding Balance: Fitness and Training for a Lifetime.* Princeton, N.J.: Princeton Book Company.

Chmelar, Robin D., and Sally S. Fitt. (1990). *Diet: A Complete Guide to Nutrition and Weight Control.* Princeton, N.J.: Princeton Book Company.

Clarkson, Priscilla M., and Margaret Skrinar. (1988). *Science of Dance Training.* Champaign, Ill.: Human Kinetics Books.

Fitt, Sally Sevey. (1996). *Dance Kinesiology.* New York: Schirmer Books, Division of Macmillan.

Howse, Justin, and Shirley Hancock. (1992). *Dance Technique and Injury Prevention.* New York: Theatre Arts Books.

Ryan, Allan J., and Robert E. Stephens. (1988). *The Dancer's Complete Guide to Healthcare and a Long Career.* Princeton, N.J.: Princeton Book Company.

Solomon, Ruth, John Solomon, and Sandra Minton, eds. (1990). *Preventing Dance Injuries: An Interdisciplinary Approach.* Reston, Va.: American Alliance for Health, Physical Education, Recreation, and Dance.

Vincent, L. M. (1979). *The Dancer's Book of Health.* Kansas City, Mo.: Sheed Andrews and McMeel, Subsidiary of Universal Press Syndicate.

Vincent, L. M. (1989). *Competing with the Sylph: The Quest for the Perfect Dance Body,* 2d ed. A Dance Horizons Book. Princeton, N. J.: Princeton Book Company.

Watkins, Andrea, and Priscilla M. Clarkson. (1990). *Dancing Longer, Dancing Stronger: A Dancer's Guide to Improving Technique and Preventing Injury.* Princeton, N.J.: Princeton Book Company.

HISTORY

Anderson, Jack. (1992). *Ballet & Modern Dance: A Concise History,* 2d ed. Princeton, N.J.: Princeton Book Company.

Au, Susan. (1988). *Ballet and Modern Dance.* New York: Thames and Hudson.

Cohen, Selma Jean. (1992). *Dance as a Theatre Art: Source Readings in Dance History from 1581 to the Present.* Princeton, N.J.: Princeton Book Company.

Jowitt, Deborah. (1989). *Time and the Dancing Image.* Berkeley: University of California Press.

Kraus, Richard G., et al. (1991). *The History of Dance in Art and Education,* 3d ed. Englewood Cliffs, N.J.: Prentice Hall Publishers.

Martin, John. (1980). *The Modern Dance.* Salem, N.H.: Ayer Publishing.

Mazo, Joseph H. (1983). *Prime Movers: The Makers of Modern Dance in America.* Princeton, N.J.: Princeton Book Company.

Ruyter, Nancy Lee Chalfa. (1979). *Reformers and Visionaries: The Americanization of the Art of Dance.* New York: Dance Horizons.

Solomon, Ruth, and John Solomon. (1995). *East Meets West in Dance Voices in the Cross-Cultural Dialogue.* New York: Harwood Academic Publishers.

CHOREOGRAPHY AND IMPROVISATION

Blom, Lynne Anne, and L. Tarin Chaplin. (1988). *The Moment of Movement.* Pittsburgh: University of Pittsburgh Press.

Hawkins, Alma M. (1991). *Moving from Within: A New Method for Dance Making.* Chicago: A Capella Books, Inc.

Minton, Sandra Cerny. (1986). *Choreography: A Basic Approach Using Improvisation.* Champaign, Ill.: Human Kinetics Publishers.

Morgenroth, Joyce. (1987). *Dance Improvisations.* Pittsburgh: University of Pittsburgh Press.

Smith, Jacqueline M. (1985). *Dance Composition: A Practical Guide for Teachers.* London: A & C Black.

EVALUATION AND CRITICISM

Croce, Arlene. (1982). *Going to the Dance.* New York: Alfred A. Knopf.

Jowitt, Deborah. (1985). *The Dance in Mind: Profiles and Reviews, 1977–83.* Boston, Mass.: David R. Godin Publishing.

Siegel, Marcia B. (1985). *The Shapes of Change: Images of American Dance.* Berkeley: University of California Press.

Terry, Walter. (1982). *How to Look at Dance.* New York: William Morrow & Company.

MISCELLANEOUS

Brown, Ann Kipling, and Monica Parker. (1984). *Dance Notation for Beginners.* London: Dance Books.

Chujoy, Anatole, and P. W. Manchester, eds. (1967). *The Dance Encyclopedia.* New York: Simon & Schuster.

Dell, Cecily. (1967). *A Primer for Movement Description.* New York: Dance Notation Bureau, Center for Movement Research and Analysis.

DuPont, Betty, and Joan Schlaich, eds. (1977). *Dance: The Art of Production.* St. Louis: Mosby.

Horosko, Marian, and Judith R. F. Kupersmith. (1987). *The Dancer's Survival Manual.* New York: Harper & Row.

Jacobs, Ellen. (1981). *Dancing: A Guide for the Dancer You Can Be.* New York: A Danceways Book.

Nielsen, Eric Brandt. (1984). *Dance Auditions*. Princeton, N.J.: Princeton Book Company.

VIDEO AND FILM

Dance Film and Video Guide
Compiled and edited by Deirdre Towers (*Footnotes* 1997, Issue No. 32)
Available from:
Performing Arts Buyers Guide
2000 Hamilton St., Suite C200
Philadelphia, PA 19105
Modern Dance and Ballet on Film and Video: A Catalog
Available from:
Dance Film Association, Inc.
1133 Broadway, Rm. 507
New York, NY 10010
Phone (212) 727-0764
Teaching Dance Improvisation
Ririe-Woodbury Dance Company
Capitol Theatre
50 W. 200 S.
Salt Lake City, UT 84101
Phone: (801) 323-6801

ON-LINE SOURCES

The Internet
Many dance companies now have Web sites where one can find information about the company and its philosophy, the performers, performance dates, and related information.

PERIODICALS

Ballett International (focuses on European dance)
P.O. Box 27 04 43
Richard-Wagner-Str. 33
D-5000 Köln 1
Dance Magazine (published monthly)
10 Columbus Circle
New York, NY 10019
Dance Magazine: College Guide
10 Columbus Circle
New York, NY 10019
Dance Research Journal (published biannually)
CORD, Dance Dept., Educ. 684D
New York University
35 W. 4th St.
New York, NY 10003
Dance Teacher Now (nine publications yearly)
P.O. Box 1074
Davis, CA 95617

Photo Credits

Title Page   Bebe Miller Dance Company, *Tiny Sisters in the Enormous Land,* Dancer: Sarah Gamblin. Photo © Lois Greenfield, 1995.

Chapter 1   Bebe Miller Company, *The Hendrix Project,* Dancers: Colleen Thomas, Bebe Miller, Anthony Phillips, Frances Craig. Photo © Lois Greenfield, 1995.

Chapter 2   Momix Baseball, Photo by Moses Pendleton.

Chapter 3   Lar Lubovitch Dance Company, *So In Love,* Choreography: Lar Lubovitch, Dancers: Dick Platzek and Sylvia Nevjinsky. Photo © Lois Greenfield, 1994.

Chapter 4   Penrod Plastino Movement Theater, *Sonata for Two,* Dancers: James Penrod and Janice G. Plastino. Photo by Donald Bradburn.

Chapter 5   Lewitzky Dance Company, *Episode #1 (Recuerdo),* Dancers: Nancy Lanier, Diane Vivona, and Lori McWilliams. Photo by Vic Luke. Pages 56-57 Isadora Duncan, Ruth St. Denis, Ted Shawn, Doris Humphrey and Charles Weidman, Martha Graham, Merce Cunningham from Dance Collection, The New York Public Library for the Performing Arts, Astor, Lenox and Tilden Foundations; Used by permission of Bella Lewitzky; Alvin Ailey, Photo © Bob Green; Alwin Nikolais, Nikolais/Lewis Foundation and Basil Langton.

Chapter 6   Bill T. Jones/Arnie Zane Dance Company, *Still/Here,* (1994). Photo © Johan Elbers.

Chapter 7   Mark Morris Dance Group, *Dido and Aeneas.* Photo by D. Pierre.

Chapter 8   Donald McKayle Dance Company, *Rainbow 'Round my Shoulder,* Choreography: Donald McKayle, Dancers: Donald McKayle and Carmen DeLavallade.

Index

Page references in italic type indicate a photograph.